THE
GIFT

THE CROP CIRCLES DECIPHERED

T H E
GIFT

THE CROP CIRCLES DECIPHERED

DOUG RUBY

BLUE NOTE BOOKS
F L O R I D A

© Copyright 1995, 1997 Doug Ruby

SECOND PRINTING

Published by Blue Note Books
a division of Blue Note Publications, Inc.
110 Polk Ave., Suite 3
Cape Canaveral, Florida 32920
For additional copies send $32.95 (includes postage)
to above address or call 1-800-624-0401

ISBN No. 1-878398-14-8

Printed in the United States of America

10 9 8 7 6 5 4 3 2

Dedication

To the creators of the crop circles and humanity.

On a personal level
to "Ma", Aunt Grace and Aunt Louise.

Acknowledgments

The cover of this book does not contain the author's name. The reason is twofold. First, we would not have the crop circles if it were not for their creators. Therefore, to a great extent, this is their book. Second, although the task of decipherment fell directly upon me, it required the input of a small group of key individuals to bring this knowledge to you. This was a team effort. Therefore, the participants who directly played a part in producing this work are presented in the order in which they appeared, as there is no special order — we are all equal.

The Participants:
Decipherer, Doug Ruby
Model maker, Al Smith
Diagrams, Fred Rose
Ship model painter, Rick Nelson

Photos, Rob Downey
Editor, Ron Van Dyke
Publisher, Paul Maluccio
Editor, Robert B. Boardman
Cover Illustrator, James Adams

I would like to extend a special "Thank you" to the following:
Alick Bartholomew, Gateway Books
Frances Gordon, Gothic Image
Publications
Then there is my girlfriend, Jeannie, who was there from the very beginning. Thank you, Jeannie, for your patience and consideration over the many months when you didn't understand what I was doing yet supported me.

- Doug Ruby

**From "Harbingers of World Change".
By Isabelle Kingston, a sensitive
living in the Avebury area of England.**

"*The satellites given — the small circles — contain the code that will be understood. Although the great shapes show signs of power, as always the smaller gems contain the greatest light. These formations came before your planet was as it is now. The formations are like molecular structures and blue prints — like a form of Morse Code — and someone will be used to unravel this information, and scientists will be able to use it and put it into practice. It will be possible to use this new form of energy within your lifetimes — in seventeen summers [from 1990]. The unraveling will start before then.*

The new source of energy is now being created, and certain beings are being prepared to understand the messages being projected at this time. Some Scientists are very close to the answer — an energy machine. This energy is only partially linked to magnetism. It is linked to the illusion of time. Rather like thought-transference, man will be able to change the molecular structure of things, including himself. Within the energy-pattern of the circles we give you this information. You humans do not believe your dreams and inspirations, so other methods have to be used. This will happen by the right people being drawn into the understanding. Some of you will be necessary to sit at the sidelines injecting love and light, and only a few will be involved totally".

Contents

Preface

This book is about crop circles and the amazing messages painstakingly recorded in the fields of farmers on four continents. Although most of those we discuss appeared in England, others have appeared in the United States, Brazil and Japan — and probably other places, where they have gone unreported.

I believe that the crop circles are a graphic form of communication from extraterrestrials — ETs, if you like. To this day, however, I have never seen an actual crop circle. My background, in retrospect, does lend itself to understanding the crop circles. After college I was a pilot in the United States Air Force, and I have been a commercial airline pilot for the past twenty-four years. Thus, I have been involved for many years in complex aircraft systems and have had extensive training in problem solving.

While I did find the subject fascinating a couple of years earlier through watching television programs and documentaries, I had written it off as a hoax — probably following Arthur C. Clark's exposè showing the truth about how they were made. I was only mildly interested in the paranormal, and completely uninvolved in metaphysical studies or activities. So why me? How did I become so involved that I would write a book?

It all started with a book — but I don't want to get ahead of myself. Let me just say that most of the information I have learned about crop circles came from a number of books. The most prominent being *Dowsing The Crop Circles, Harbingers of World Change,* and *The Crop Circle Enigma.* The first of these books concentrates solely on the dowsers and their findings, while the latter two encompass the entire phenomena. Since the authors and publisher of these two books did not know what direction the subject would ultimately go, they used an organized shotgun strategy.

All imaginable sources of information pertaining to the crop circles were presented with the thought in mind that someone would ultimately find the key to the puzzle. With that key the pieces would start coming together, allowing discovery of the answer to the mystery, the meaning of these formations in the fields. Their philosophy was correct, and I strongly recommend these books to the interested reader. They are presented extremely well, and I have analyzed them exhaustively.

The duty seems to have fallen upon me to painstakingly gather the pellets from the shotgun blasts and place them in an order that would lead to a greater understanding. This was not easily accomplished, as you will soon discover. However, I believe I have found the key to unlocking the door to this enigma.

It is not my intention to repeat information found in other sources, except where it is absolutely necessary. What I will do is present the story, step by step, regarding my own involvement and insights. The path to my discoveries was not always easy, but it was always interesting. It took patience as I was led to the point of greater understanding. Much repetition was required before the obvious could be seen and understood. While I have tried to eliminate as much of this repetition as possible, repetition is the key to learning. That is why, I believe, similar patterns emerged repeatedly with a new twist applied to each. They were trying to tell us, "Look at this! There's a message here!"

I believe the crop circles comprise a multilayered maze intentionally presented to confuse anyone trying to decipher them. It was meant to be a challenge. It's a puzzle equivalent to the pyramids, or to Stonehenge. The answer, however, lies in simple, basic, common sense. It is nothing more than logic. The most complex mathematics required was basic algebra. If A = B and B = C, then A = C; therefore A + B + C = D (where D equals the summation of A, B, C). Even though this was the case, I sometimes struggled for days or even weeks to get the message. Once I saw it, though, it seemed so obvious. It just seemed to click. Still, it took much organization on my part to discover the patterns that were emerging.

For the most part, I worked alone, sharing my insights with only a few key people who helped me build the models, take the pictures, and make the drawings. At one point I also consulted an electrical engineer to clarify some things for me. What I have tried to do in writing this book is to present the subject in a concise and straightforward manner. A youngster in a middle school or junior high science class should have little difficulty understanding most of what is presented. It will be interesting, in fact, to see if youngsters with uncluttered and fresh minds see things that I may have missed. I sincerely hope so, and also hope some scientists will take my findings further than I have been able to go. In any case, I ask that you keep your mind as open as possible. I do not claim to have the final word. Remember that this material breaks new ground. It is, I believe, a key to opening up more of the universe to our greater understanding. If my work advances this goal, I will surely be most delighted.

Introduction

Throughout our history we have always wondered if we are alone in the vast cosmos. Most of that time we have been incapable of space flight, stranded on our emerald planet, capable only of peering out in awe at the night sky and the immense galaxy floating above.

Our questions are of such abundance that we are like children asking a million of them all at once, only to discover that no one is there to answer. At long last our wait is over. We have company!

Our company has meticulous manners. They have chosen to introduce themselves by offering us an absolutely unbelievable gift. Incredibly, our gift is a starship capable of crossing the Milky Way.

They have chosen to offer their gift to all the peoples of our planet. This has been indicated by their presenting it in the form of drawings that are placed in farmers' fields for all to view. We call these drawings crop circles.

Amazingly, as they drew their diagrams in the fields, not one stalk of grain was ever harmed. Each stalk was gently bent but never broken. Thus, they have exhibited a great respect for our planet, for us and for all life, right down to a stalk of grain. Through their actions they have conveyed a very strong message to us. The message is that they are gentle and extremely respectful beings.

Our visitors are also considerate beings. By introducing their gift in the form of a puzzle, they knew it would require a certain amount of time before someone deciphered the crop circles and solved the puzzle. It has been five years since the crop circles were created in abundance and our attention first became focused upon them. This has allowed us time to gradually accept the notion that perhaps, just perhaps, we have visitors.

It is as if they are telling us, "Relax, there is no rush and nothing to fear. We experienced this same situation ourselves a long time ago and undestand perfectly what you are going through. You have received our gift and know that we are considerate and gentle beings. You also know that our gift is one of love and respect for you, for your planet, and for all life upon it."

Like the children with a million questions, let's unwrap our gift.

CHAPTER ONE

The Little Yellow Book

It is Sunday afternoon, January 1, 1994. My girlfriend Jeannie and I are browsing through our favorite bookstore. We always split up on such occasions, as she is a grazing shopper, while I, like most men, move quickly. Contentedly alone and moving rapidly through the book racks, I am discovering absolutely nothing of interest. It is occurring to me that my search for whatever might end up in one of those desperation purchases. Now there is nothing wrong with a desperation purchase, except for the short dissertation that I will receive about my lousy shopping habits. This is always a difficult pill to swallow.

Suddenly, I am saved by a little yellow book that has leapt off the shelf and smacked me right between the eyes. Its title is **Dowsing The Crop Circles.** After quickly scanning the book, I noted that, except for the front and back covers, there were no photos of the crop circles. However, there were numerous scale drawings. (Little did I know how invaluable these drawings would prove in the future.) I recalled

that the crop circles were mainly created in a particular area of England that was, more or less, centered about an ancient megalithic site known as Stonehenge. I remembered how interesting crop circles had seemed before I learned that they were hoaxes created by a couple of pranksters. Like many other folks my interest had rapidly dissipated. Since I had some early experience with dowsing, I thought this book would at least be an interesting diversion. Could dowsing prove authenticity or confirm that they were, indeed, mere hoaxes? The book was perfect, just what I was looking for.

Now, where is Jeannie? Again, I have demonstrated the advantages of rapid shopping. I scurry through the book racks searching for her. It is imperative that I quickly find her so I can deliver my short dissertation, "I'm finished! Are you ready yet?" Oh, how I love these moments!

The trip home was one of laughter and bantering about our divergent shopping habits. We enjoy kidding each other, and this was a perfect occasion for good-natured joking.

Once home, I quickly settled into my favorite couch to investigate my new book. The book, as I said, was about dowsers and their findings within the crop circles. Webster's dictionary defines dowse as, "To search for water or minerals by means of a divining rod (origin unknown)." Dowsers are an independent lot whose abilities lie at the fringes of our so-called scientific society. Although I have never had much interest in the paranormal or metaphysical, I did realize there were things out there that were simply inexplicable. In other words, I had an open mind. Besides, I had experienced dowsing as a youngster while helping my uncle dig a well for a camp he was building.

When it came time to dig the well, my uncle invited a friend of his over to look for water with him. My uncle explained to me that his friend was a dowser. When this fellow arrived, he cut and trimmed a tree branch that was shaped like a Y. Grasping the branch with one fork in each hand and holding it horizontally in front of himself, he proceeded to walk around my uncle's property. Suddenly the branch bent over towards the earth, and the two of them marked the spot. These proceedings continued until a particular spot was decided upon. Naturally, I was right there observing all of this and asked if I could give it a try. It worked! I was amazed at the strength that the branch exuded when it took one of its nose dives.

Well, these dowsers in *Dowsing The Crop Circles* were dowsing for something different from water or minerals. They were dowsing for energy lines and had been doing this for quite some time. They lived in an area of England that is alive with energy lines. Most of these energy lines are located within a hundred mile radius of Stonehenge, interconnecting the many ancient religious sites. It was at about this point that I recognized that something was going on, because the dowsers stated that they could authenticate a crop circle within a couple of minutes after entering it. In other words, they could tell a real crop circle from a hoax within a couple of minutes! They did this by feeling the energy within a genuine crop circle as well as by having their metal Y-shaped rods take off on them, just as the tree branch had done in my hands years ago. The man-made crop circles, or hoaxes, did not exhibit these qualities.

The dowsers went on to say that they could not stay in a freshly-formed crop circle for very long, as they would become dizzy, light headed, and confused. Furthermore, common people visiting a fresh crop circle exhibited the same symptoms. When I added up what I had just learned, it became obvious that something was going on here, and it was not about hoaxes. I am sure my experience with a divining rod as a youngster helped me to validate the dowsers' statements. I knew dowsing worked because there was water beneath the spot that my uncle and his dowser friend selected.

This little yellow book, *Dowsing The Crop*

Circles, spurred me on to investigate crop circles further. Returning to the book store, I ordered more books about crop circles; two being *Harbingers of World Change* and *The Crop Circle Enigma.* These provided me with a wealth of information. Photographs and diagrams abounded, as well as a comprehensive discussion about the phenomenon.

As I read these books, I learned that the crop circles began appearing in small numbers during the 1970's. In the 1980's their numbers increased to thirty or forty a year. No one knows an exact number, as many times they were simply mowed down by the farmers with their harvesting machines.

Then, in 1988 there were approximately fifty, followed in 1989 by a hundred. Interestingly, all of these crop circles were circular in form. It was about this time that folks began to take serious notice of these strange formations. All sorts of theories were formulated as to their origin. They ran the gamut from whirlwinds to time warps to secret military operations. All of these explanations were based on one constant feature of all the crop circles. They were all circular in form.

The summer of 1990 blew every conceivable theory away. Three things occurred.

First, there were approximately one thousand crop circles created. Second, the crop circles changed in form from circles to complex shapes. Third, the diagrams were of immense size, with many over a hundred yards long. These three events received worldwide circulation.

Then, near the end of the summer of 1991, two local people announced that they had been making the crop circles and pronounced them to be hoaxes. All interest, including my own, died as this was publicized.

In direct contradiction to my earlier conclusion, I was quickly learning through these books that the crop circles were for real. They were not hoaxes. What really won me over was a short dissertation contained in *Harbingers of World Change.* It was about a concerted, scientific attempt to discover, photograph and record the creation of the crop circles and their creators. After reading it, I had taken the bait — hook, line, and sinker. The subject would consume me for over a year, changing the way I see many things.

THE PLOT THICKENS

As reported in *Harbingers of World Change,* John Macnish and David Morgenstern ran a surveillance operation known as *Project Chameleon* in the Summer of 1991. This operation followed *Operation Blackbird* run by BCC Pebble Mill and Bratton in 1990. It was located on Morgan's Hill near Devizes in England. They set up banks of expensive cameras and infrared equipment to overlook the same field where an awesome, quadruple-ringed circle appeared on June 1, 1990, followed by a Celtic cross on July 5 in the same year.

Besides the video equipment, powerful directional microphones were pointed at the field. Operating with a range of 2-40,000

Hz, all sound in the field would be recorded. The range included infrasound, audible sound, and some ultrasound. In addition, intruder alarm equipment was set up at both entrance points to the field by Mike Carrie, director of Cloud 9, a security system marketing company. Anyone entering from either direction would trigger warning indicators. Further, a remote controlled *Skystalk* television camera was mounted by Cloud 9 on a 150-foot arm to scan the entire area, including both entrances. Any movement would be detected. With all these various sensors, unobserved access to the field was virtually impossible.

The dedication of these crop circle watchers paid off the night of June 28-29, 1991. Even though it was cloudy and damp all evening, with an unusually heavy fog and mist moving in about 3:00 a.m., they decided to keep the equipment running. It was not until around 6:00 a.m. that the unseasonable fog began to dissipate. Then finally, as the dawn broke, the mist cleared. They could not believe their eyes as they viewed new markings in the field.

Rushing down the hill, they saw a dumbbell formation with circles of unequal size. How could it be? There was no sign of entry, not even footprints in the wet soil. All recordings were completely blank at all frequencies.

The editor of *Harbingers of World Change* said, "I spoke to Mike Carrie, who was first into the dumbbell formation. He had walked a long way along a tram-line to get there without damaging the standing crop. His trousers were soaked by the wet crop and his boots covered in mud. The circles were perfectly swirled, with the crops bent but unbroken. There was no sign of footprints or muddy tramplings in the circles.

He said, 'When I was at Blackbird last year I really thought all you people were daft, and the circles were man-made. Now I just don't know what to think.' He and the others who were there that night were puzzled and rather thoughtful. It was just as if a conjurer had spread a large silk handkerchief in front of them, waved his hands, and then produced from under it a magical white rabbit. Only this cosmic conjurer was himself invisible."

CHAPTER TWO

Deciphering The Crop Circles

By the time I had finished reading the last of my books, I was convinced that an unknown intelligence was attempting to communicate with us without revealing itself. I figured that the next logical step for me to take would be to investigate the crop circles themselves. As I looked at the photos and diagrams contained in my crop circle books, it occurred to me that something had been missed in the many attempts to decipher these formations. After all, the crop circles had now been with us for over three years and no one had come close to deciphering them.

For the next few days I reflected on how another civilization would initiate communication with us, or with any other civilization, for that matter. This line of thought led me to the training being done with dolphins and orcas. Here I saw man communicating with another species very effectively, although neither knew the other's verbal language. It was all done with hand signals that were the equiva-

lent of visual communication. The crop circles were also visual communication. I felt that I had established a common denominator.

It was now a matter of placing my mind within those of the trainer and the dolphins or orcas. Obviously, communication must have evolved from very basic hand signals into the complex. This process would require a series of steps to be taken that would lead up to a hand signal that a dolphin or orca would interpret as a request to do a double flip rather than a single flip. It also became apparent that during this learning period a relationship between the trainers and the dolphins or orcas would be established. In other words, they would get to know each another.

When I applied these thoughts to the crop circles, it immediately became apparent what everyone had missed. All attention was being focused on the dolphin-orca show with no consideration given to the months or years of steady communication that had transpired to produce it. In other words, everyone had been looking for the complex and bypassed the simple, basic communication that must first occur before confronting the complex. I concluded that within the simplest of the crop circles lay the instructions to decipher the more complex diagrams.

With this thought in mind I began searching for the simplest of the crop circles. I settled on a double-ringer that was formed on the Longwood Estate.

The crop circles were individually named under two names. The first was derived from the location where the crop circle was formed, and the second from what the crop circle formation looked like to the investigators. Thus, some crop circles have two names, while others have just one.

THE DOUBLE-RINGER AT LONGWOOD ESTATE
created June 6, 1990

Photo No. 1: Model Stationary   **Photo No. 2**: Model Spinning

THE DOUBLE-RINGER AT LONGWOOD ESTATE

As I looked at a photo of this crop circle, I kept reminding myself to look for the simple and the obvious. I also attempted to place my mind within the intelligence that had created the crop circles. What would they want me to do with this thing? For starters, this crop circle was big! The diameter of the circle was ninety-six feet. Obviously the photo had been taken from the air.

For me to observe this crop circle, I would either have to be in an airplane or be a giant. One other alternative occurred to me. I could make the crop circle smaller. If I did this, I would become the giant in the field. So I made a three-inch disc of the crop circle and drew in the interrupted rings (See Photo 1). With the disc in my hand, I decided to place it back in the field by tossing it onto the floor. As I looked at the little disc a thought occurred to me. Suppose I was walking along outside somewhere, anywhere, and came across this object lying on the ground. What would my reaction be? First, I would wonder what it was; then I would bend over, pick it up, and examine it at close range. I picked up the disk and did something without thinking. I flipped it up in the air and simultaneously spun it with my hand. This spinning action caused the interrupted rings to appear solid (See Photo 2). I remarked to myself that it was just like a child's top. A rounded button was glued to the center on the back of the disc; then I flipped it onto my dining room table to see if it would spin. It did. The interrupted rings formed continuous rings just as they had done previously, only much better.

This three-inch, spinning disc was the portal through which I entered the crop circles. I deduced four things from my encounter with this crop circle:

1) I was correct in my approach to the crop circles. The answers would lie in the simple and the obvious. All that I had to do was pick the crop circles up by making small models of them and they would lead me to the answers.

2) Just as with the case of the trainer and the dolphins and orcas, the simpler crop circles contained the instructions to decipher the complex ones.

3) This crop circle had a very straightforward message. The models were meant to be spun.

4) The creators of the crop circles were communicating through basic logic and common sense. This deduction led me to a casual observation that would be validated frequently. These beings know us very well. Just as we studied the dolphins and orcas before arriving at a method of communication, so have they. You will see over and over throughout our journey into the crop circles that they were designed for a human mind to comprehend.

It was time to choose another crop circle and again I decided to stick with the simplest that I could find.

THE SIX PETALED FLOWER AT CHILCOMB DOWN
created in late July, 1991

Photo No. 3: Model Stationary   **Photo No. 4**: Model Spinning

In 1991, the creators of the crop circles changed from simple linear and circular displays to more complex patterns. One of the new forms was the *Six Petaled Flower.* The first of these appeared at Chilcomb Down. These *Six Petaled Flower* crop circles have a unique history. This history is reported in ***Harbingers of World Change.*** Because I find it quite interesting, I will summarize it here.

Six investigators decided to see if they could produce a circle of a particular design through meditation. A six-pointed design like the Star of David was the objective. Placing a hexagonal crystal in the center, they lay on the ground positioning themselves equally around it with their feet pointing inward.

Nothing happened in that field that night; but as they prepared to leave the next morning, a man came into the field and asked if they had seen the new circle. They went with him to an adjoining field and saw a six petaled flower formation that had appeared during the

12

night. It was not the Star of David they had tried to produce, but it was very similar.

Then, about one week later, a second six petaled flower, larger than the first and surrounded by double rings, appeared. It showed up in the same field where six people sat and heard mysterious trilling noises about two years earlier, on June 18, 1989. This had been reported in *The Crop Circle Enigma.*

Perhaps these were mere coincidences, but for those who were personally involved it was quite meaningful. In each case there were six people and six points. It was certainly thought provoking.

Afterwards, hoaxers claimed to have made this formation, like many others. However, two individuals, Richard Andrews and Leonie Starr, were crop-watching the night the great flower appeared. They did not see or hear anything; but the next morning they were approached by a man who had been driving by around 2:00 a.m.. He was returning to see if the dome of light he saw moving over the field as he drove by had created a new crop circle. The others had seen nothing, but had heard his car pass at 2:00 a.m..

One more point of interest: when the dowsers checked this circle, the energy readings showed it to be genuine.

As we discuss this *Six Petaled Flower* crop circle, notice how the crop circle creators nudged me towards another discovery, namely, the incorporation of a shaft. I began by making a small model of the disc and attached the two eyebrows to it as depicted in the crop circle (See Photo 3). Naturally, the disc is not going to spin very well as the eyebrows place it in an unbalanced state. To solve this minor problem the disc was mounted on a wooden dowel. Now the dowel could be rolled between my hands to spin the disc. After spinning it a few times that way, it became apparent that there was still too much interfering motion. The solution was to make a machine with which I could spin the shaft and disc. This required me to leave the crop circles for a couple of days to design and build a spinning machine.

I ended up building a wooden box, minus two of its sides, and incorporating legs into the structure. A fan motor was then attached beneath the box and a hole drilled in the top to accommodate the disc's shaft. This enabled me to slip a shaft through the top hole and into a receptacle on the end of the fan-motor shaft. With the addition of a rheostat, the project was finished. The spinning machine worked perfectly, allowing me to see what the *Six Petaled Flower* model looked like when spun at various speeds.

As you can see in Photo 4, the eyebrows transform into something entirely different from their stationary appearance and expand the disc's size considerably. They were doing this by adding two additional transparent rings to the model. It was obvious to me that the crop circle was conveying two pieces of information.

1) Again, the models were definitely intended to be spun.
2) When the models were spun, their appear-

ance underwent a metamorphosis that revealed the information to be communicated.

With these thoughts in mind, I decided to take a look at another crop circle.

GREAT WISHFORD
created mid July, 1990

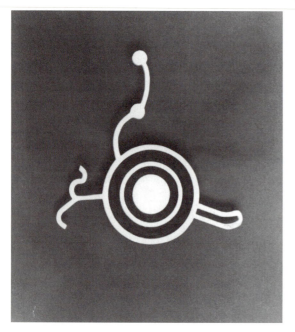

Photo No. 5: Model Stationary

Photo No. 6: Model Spinning

This crop circle is just slightly more complex than the *Six Petaled Flower;* and as I attempted to make a model, another problem arose. My models, previously created of cardboard, required a stronger material due to the centrifugal forces placed upon them while spinning. A fine grade of plywood appeared to be the answer except that I did not possess the required tools, nor the space to accommodate them.

Jeannie, who was now visibly shaking at the prospect of losing the last semblance of an apartment, appropriately suggested a carpenter. Her suggestion prompted me to search for someone who had both the time and the ability to make my models for me. This led me to a warehouse subdivided into a number of bays occupied by craftsmen of all types. I noticed a fellow in front of his woodworking shop who appeared to be waiting for someone. I approached him and started talking; but when he asked me what I was making, an obvious question, it caught me totally off guard. I realized I was unprepared to make anyone a confidant. How much could I tell him? What would he think? Thoughts raced through my mind as I debated how much to say. I simply ended up blurting out the truth. "I want you to make models of crop circles," I said. His reply left me speechless—"You're right on time," he said.

It was as if he was expecting me, which, months later, he confirmed. (He said afterward that he had wondered what took me so long.) He left me scratching my head that day — and many times since — with his uncanny remarks. What more can I say? It was a perfect fit. Al Smith is not only a patient master carpenter, but he has also become a good friend. As he and I traversed and discussed the crop circles together, we became almost inseparable. He meticulously and patiently crafted all the models pictured in this book. He cut and sanded, while I assembled them and did the painting. Since the crop circle creators never stipulated a color scheme, I chose one of black and white for contrast.

Now let's return to the *Great Wishford* formation. Photo 6 is of the disc spinning. The three appendages are creating a number of transparent rings that are giving the effect of looking into a spinning cone. Besides this observation, there does not appear to be anything else to be gleaned from this crop circle model.

It is becoming apparent to me that the program is moving at a snail's pace and I am becoming impatient. I decide to diverge from the simple formations and jump over to the big boys — the pictograms.

CHAPTER THREE

The Pictograms

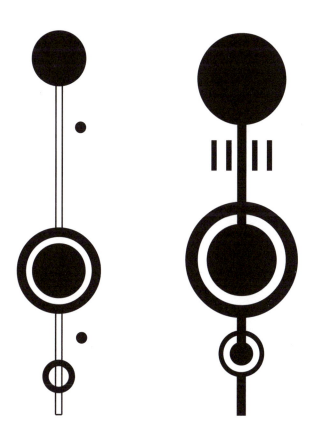

ALTON BARNES AND CRAWLEY

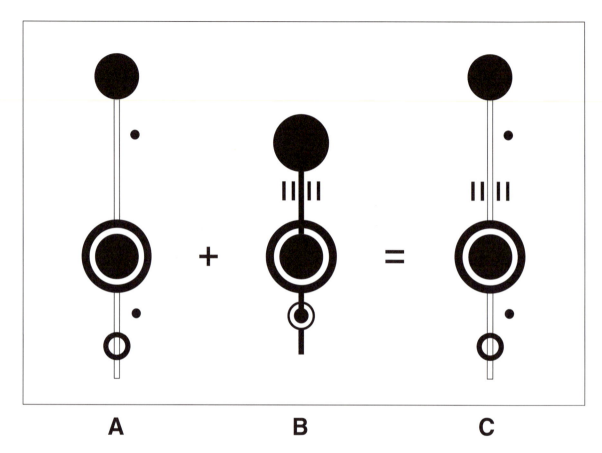

A   **B**   **C**

Diagram No. 1: Combining *Alton Barnes* and *Crawley* formations

A) Diagram of the *Alton Barnes* crop circle as it appeared in the field.
B) Diagram of the *Crawley* crop circle as it appeared in the field.
C) The combination of features from the *Alton Barnes* and *Crawley* formations. Note that only the spacers from the *Crawley* formation were transferred to the *Alton Barnes* formation.

I just finished introducing Al, one of the key players, to you. Now I would like to introduce you to another who has also been invaluable to me in this work.

Fred Rose is the gentleman who created all the diagrams in this book. As the two of us progressed through the crop circles it became obvious that the formations were originally created on a computer. As soon as Fred has finished helping me get this book into print, he is going to create a video of all of these formations and their resultant models. He will then animate them for you and lead you through the crop circles by way of computer. I believe it would have been the crop circle creator's first choice in presenting them to you.

Take a look at Diagram 1A. It is a scale diagram of the *Alton Barnes* crop circle. As you can see, the formation is of much greater complexity than the circular ones that we have just encountered. It exemplifies the type of formations that began appearing during the summer of 1990. The English named these complex crop circles pictograms. I chose this pictogram as it appeared to be the most straightforward of the lot.

Alton Barnes was the first pictogram ever created, and it has been recreated many times. In fact, nine days after this formation was formed, a duplicate appeared in a nearby field with its size doubled. Reflecting back on this, I believe the creators, by doubling the size, were drawing special attention to it, as if they were saying, "Start here with this one." It is, as you shall see, the most important of all the crop circles, although I was not aware of this at the time.

Returning to Diagram 1, notice that the formation depicted in 1B is almost identical to the *Alton Barnes* formation in 1A. The only difference between the two is that Diagram 1A has two floating circles off to one side while Diagram 1B has four rectangular boxes located near its center shaft. Figure 1B is a diagram of a crop circle that was formed at *Crawley* and is called the *Crawley* pictogram. The thought occurred to me that these two very similar crop circles could be added together. To accomplish this I simply added the four rectangular boxes from Diagram 1B to Diagram 1A. The result can be seen in Diagram 1C. The combination of two pictograms might appear presumptuous, but let me assure you that the reason becomes obvious.

Diagram 2A (next page) is a copy of the *Alton Barnes/Crawley* pictogram that we just arrived at in Diagram 1. While studying this complex formation, the thought occurred to me that the moment of truth was at hand. I would either succeed in breaking the crop circle code or be concluding a wild goose chase.

I decided to approach this pictogram from my original concept and look for the simple and the obvious. Again, I mentally reviewed the pertinent observations made thus far. For starters, an intelligence was trying to communicate with us. This intelligence was communicating through flat diagrams. It was all two-dimensional. Eureka! Of course! If the diagrams were drawn with the three circles

ALTON BARNES/CRAWLEY

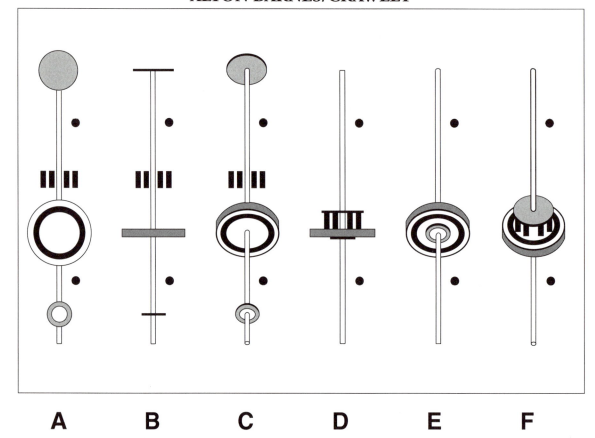

A **B** **C** **D** **E** **F**

Diagram No. 2: Combining discs to make model

A) Diagram of the *Alton Barnes/Crawley* formation depicted in Diagram 1C.
B) The three discs have been rotated ninety degrees.
C) The model depicted in B has been rotated away to allow you a view of its bottom.
D) The three discs have been moved inward. The top disc stops when it meets the
   vertical spacers. The bottom disc rests against the underside of the center disc.
E) The model depicted in D has been rotated away to allow you a view of its bottom.
F) The model depicted in D has been rotated inward to allow you a view of its top.

perpendicular to the shaft, they would appear as three lines cutting across the shaft and reveal nothing. Furthermore, I had just deciphered three crop circles, two of which required shafts to spin them. This formation contained a shaft within it! From this train of thought, I concluded that the discs must rotate ninety degrees and remain in their respective positions on the shaft. Diagram 2B depicts all three discs rotated ninety degrees, while Diagram 2C indicates the formation rotated slightly to offer you a better view of the discs.

At this point I constructed an actual model of Diagram 2C and began fiddling with it. Within a short time I had slid the two outer discs inward toward the center disc until they all met. I had made a nice little pancake. Immediately after doing this, I realized my mistake. I had forgotten to include the four rectangular blocks still remaining in the diagram. When I inserted the blocks between the upper and center discs, I had the three-dimensional picture shown in Diagram 2D. Diagram 2E depicts the model rotated slightly to allow you to view its bottom portion, and Diagram 2F depicts the model rotated in the opposite direction for you to view its top. At the time, it seemed odd that the lower disc butted right up against the center disc, but that's the way it came together. This was all correct and I knew it immediately.

Something peculiar occurs when a crop circle model is assembled. When it is correct, it just clicks together. It is amazing how it happens. The click is so perceptible that you can almost

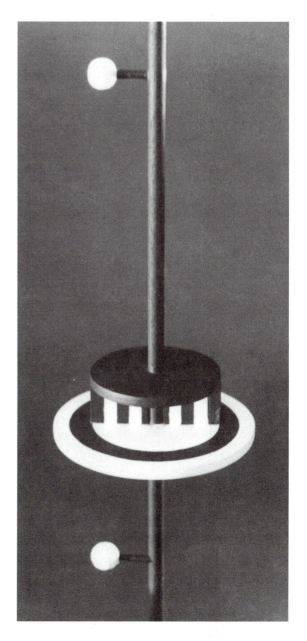

Photo No. 7: Model Stationary
(Top View)

ALTON BARNES / CRAWLEY

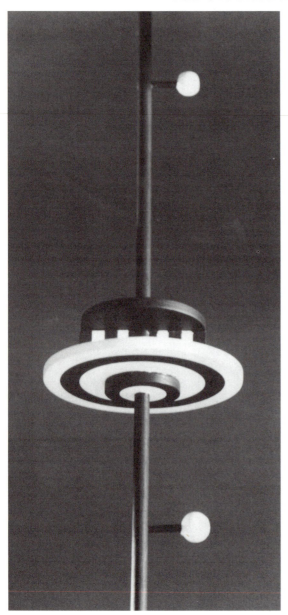 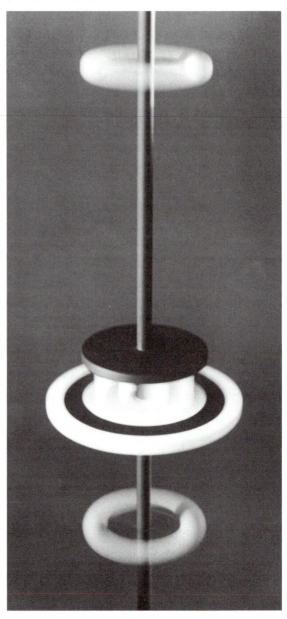

Photo No. 8: Model Stationary
(Bottom View)

Photo No. 9: Model Spinning
(Side View)

hear it. The *Alton Barnes* model clicked together. Rest assured that additional and substantial verification of the correctness of this model is forthcoming.

The only remaining pieces on the diagram were the two floating circles. Since the model was now three-dimensional, I concluded that the circles must represent spheres and attached them to the shaft at the locations indicated by the diagram. A complete model of the *Alton Barnes/Crawley* pictogram lay before me. Photos 7 and 8 are of this model.

Again, the crop circles had done the work for me. I only had to follow their unwritten instructions, and pieces of the puzzle would fall into place. I did not consider it to be coincidental that the two previous models required shafts and this model had one included with it. Obviously, the model was intended to be spun.

As I prepared to mount the model on the spinning machine, I was faced with the decision as to which end was up. What was the top and what was the bottom? Take another look at Photos 7 and 8. They depict the model in its correct attitude. If you were in my place, I believe that you would have made the same decision. It just looks correct. This common sense observation will be verified many times as we progress through the crop circles.

Photo 9 is of the model spinning. Notice that the two floating spheres have transformed into two transparent energy fields that rotate about the central shaft. These energy fields are located both above and below the model. Likewise, the four rectangular blocks between the center and upper discs are creating the illusion of a solid structure.

Notice that this model is composed of three discs. They are the top disc, the center disc and the bottom disc. Now note each disc's size in relation to the other two, as indicated in Diagram 2A. Also note the rings associated with each disc. These distinguishing features of the discs and their relationship with each other will become instrumental in deciphering future crop circles. All the crop circles will flow from this universal model that extends a chord of continuity throughout the phenomenon.

CHAPTER FOUR

The Insectograms

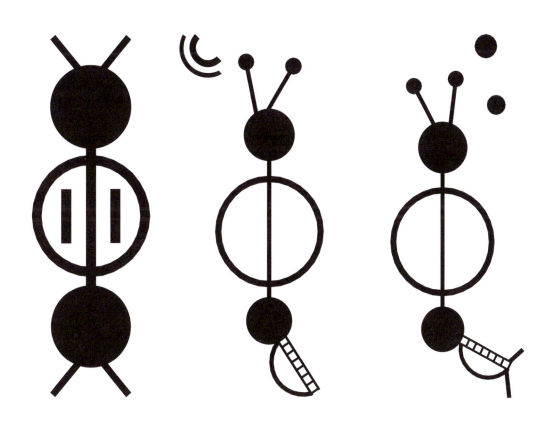

THE FIRST INSECTOGRAM: BARN HEAD
created August 11, 1990

During the early summer of 1990, many dumbbell shaped crop circles were created. The English appropriately named them dumbbells. During the later portion of this summer a few complex dumbbell formations appeared that further evolved into even more complex formations called insectograms. The crop circle creators were trying to start us off with the simple and lead us into the complex. For instance, a deciphered, plain, dumbbell formation only indicated that the discs were rotated ninety degrees. Thus, these formations were intended to be instructional tools used to decipher the more complex pictograms such as *Alton Barnes* and this forerunner of the insectograms, *Barn Head*. I had completely missed this entire step in the communication process.

Diagram 3A presents a scale drawing of the *Barn Head* pictogram. As I studied the diagram of this crop circle it became apparent that all three discs rotated ninety degrees and moved inward on the shaft to form a model. However, the two rectangular blocks in the center circle and the two antennae protruding from each smaller circle were total unknowns. *Barn Head* presented the continuity of *Alton Barnes* while simultaneously creating a puzzle of its own.

As I attempted to assemble the model it became immediately apparent that the spacers were missing, or were they? There were two rectangular blocks within the center disc (See Diagram 3A). I concluded that these two rectangular blocks rotated horizontally ninety degrees as the disc rotated ninety degrees (See

Diagram 3B). This smacked of my childhood when I would assemble a car, truck, or bus from a piece of cardboard included as a prize in a box of cereal. The big difference between the crop circle models and the cereal box models was that the latter included instructions. In this case, the rectangular blocks rotated horizontally outward and were as high as the width of the blocks. This rotation met with a perceptible click as the blocks now extended from one edge of each smaller disc to the other and constituted a perfect fit. The horizontal blocks, when rotated, had become spacers that gave the discs a depth equal to the width of the spacers. The spacers were meant to apply to both of the smaller discs. In other words, the blocks rotated to their perpendicular position both on top and below the center disc (See Diagram 3B).

The only remaining unknowns were the antennae. I just fiddled with them and before long discovered that they bent inward and snuggled up to the center shaft as if they had really missed it. In other words, when they met the shaft, another perceptible click occurred. The antennae turned out to be quite easy and concluded the assembly of *Barn Head* (See Diagram 3D, E).

It was at this time that I made another discovery simply by sitting back and thinking about what I had just accomplished. Since the crop circles were presented in only two dimensions, there really was no way to know how thick the discs were intended to be, except for the distance indicated by the spacers. Since the

BARN HEAD

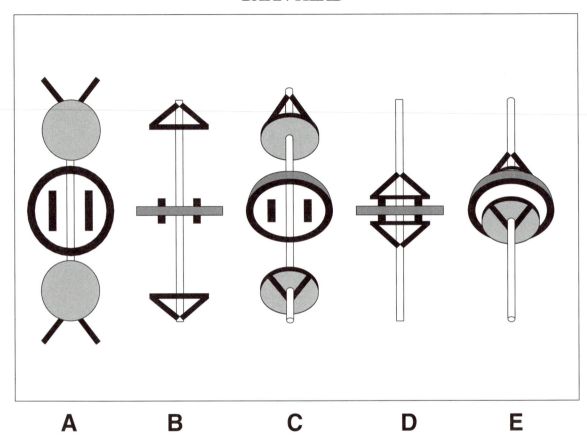

A   B   C   D   E

Diagram No. 3: Assembly of the Model

A) Diagram of the *Barn Head* crop circle as it appeared in the field.
B) The three discs have been rotated ninety degrees. When the center disk rotates ninety degrees, the spacers also rotate ninety degrees to their upright position. The antennae are actually horizontal to the two outer disks, however, they would not show if depicted in that fashion.
C) The model depicted in (B) has been rotated away to allow you a view of its bottom.
D) The three disks have been moved inward until meeting the spacers. The antennae have been rotated inward until meeting the center shaft.
E) The model shown in (D) has been rotated away to allow you a view of its bottom. The top is identical.

spacers did indicate a specific distance between the discs, it occurred to me that I could incorporate this distance within the structure of the top or bottom discs. In other words, I could make the top or bottom discs a thickness equal to the width of the spacers. Therefore, I had Al make the two smaller discs in this model the thickness of the spacers. This eliminated the spacers entirely from the finished model. You can see this in Photo 10. The thickness of the center disc is not indicated in any of the crop circles. Therefore, I arbitrarily chose a thickness for the center disc and used it throughout all the models.

With *Barn Head* deciphered and the model completed, the only thing remaining was to spin the model (See Photos 11 and 12). When spun, the most pronounced observation was the transparent energy field that the antennae formed above and below the model. Second, these energy fields have their terminuses at the vertical shaft and at the edge of their respective upper and lower disc.

Barn Head revealed the two energy fields that exist both above and below the center disc. Not coincidentally, the *Alton Barnes* model also indicated that an energy field existed both above and below the model. Although their meaning is a total mystery to me at this point, I feel that I am making steady headway through the crop circles.

BARN HEAD

Photo No. 10: Model Stationary
(Top View)

Photo No. 11: Model Spinning
(Top View)

BARN HEAD

Photo No. 12: Model Spinning
(Side View)

THE SECOND INSECTOGRAM: STONEHENGE
created July 10, 1990

The *Stonehenge* insectogram epitomizes the complex insectograms created during the summer of 1990. The formation exuded a grandness that I could not resist. I felt confident that I could decipher it. Little did I know that I had selected one of the most difficult crop circles ever created. The ladder was the problem. What was this thing? Finally, after two weeks of skull drudgery, I deciphered it. Fortunately, the crop circle was as rewarding in its revelations as it was difficult in decipherment.

Diagram 4A is a drawing of the *Stonehenge* insectogram as it lay in the field, while Diagram 4B indicates the three discs rotated ninety degrees. The top of the insectogram contains two antennae with spheres attached to their ends, as well as two floating eyebrows. All of this assembled rather easily, since I knew from the *Barn Head* insectogram that the antennae most likely folded up against the vertical shaft. When the antennae were folded onto the shaft, something amazing happened. The two eyebrows came right along with the left antenna and folded up against the center shaft to form a half sphere (See Diagram 4C). All of this clicked into position so quickly that I was simultaneously taken by surprise as well as astonished at what had just occurred. After spending a few minutes examining this handiwork of some very clever being, I realized that I was dealing with a wizard of crop circle design. My enthusiasm to discover what lay on the bottom half of this crop circle was now at a feverish pitch.

Since I had been so successful in my approach to the top of the crop circle, I decided to duplicate the process for the bottom. First, I assembled a cardboard model of the bottom portion of this crop circle and then fiddled with the ladder and half-circle until I wore it out and had to make another. This continued for a number of days with no success. Finally, I realized that something was missing. Perhaps the center disc was required for this thing to make sense. To include the center disc, a model would be required. I began to assemble one. Almost immediately a spacer problem was encountered, as there were none included with the diagram. A thought occurred to me and I returned to the previous crop circle, *Barn Head*. In the *Barn Head* diagram I noted that the horizontal spacers were the same width as the distances between the center disc and the two smaller discs (See Diagram 3A).

This had to be the answer. With it came an astute observation. The crop circle creators had inserted stopgaps within their formations that could only be overcome by proceeding through the crop circles in an orderly manner. Reverting to Diagram 4A, I noted that the distances between the upper and lower discs to the center disc were unequal. I reasoned that these distances must indicate the respective thickness of the top and bottom discs. I asked Al to cut the top and bottom discs to these measurements (See Diagram 4B).

Now things again happened rapidly and so easily that I simultaneously felt amazed and stupid. You see, once a crop circle is deciphered, the logical simplicity of it bowls you

STONEHENGE

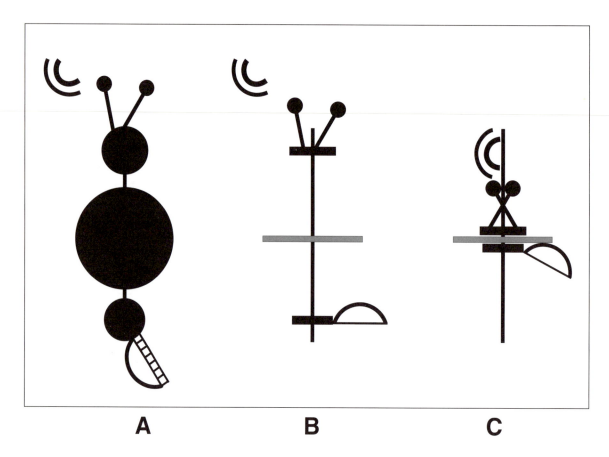

A   **B**   **C**

Diagram No. 4: Assembly

A) Diagram of the *Stonehenge* crop circle as it appeared in the field.
B) The three discs have been rotated ninety degrees.
C) The two antennae have crossed each other due to the spheres attached to their ends. When this occurs, the eyebrows move up against the center shaft. Beneath the model, the arc portion of the ladder assembly rotates ninety degrees, forcing the ladder downward at a specific angle.

STONEHENGE

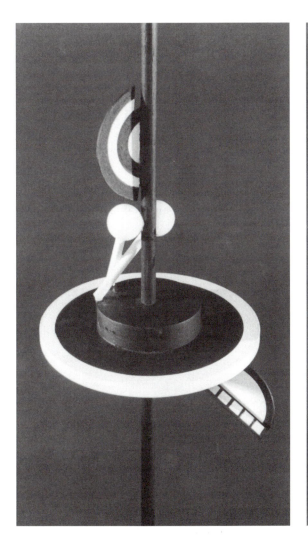 

Photo No. 13: Model Stationary
(Top View)

Photo No. 14: Model Stationary
(Side View)

over and a pronounced feeling of stupidity on your part sets in for not seeing the obvious sooner. Here is what occurred as I fiddled with the bottom of this insectogram.

With the center disc in place, my fiddling options became quite limited. Within minutes the answer lay before me (See Diagram 4C). What happened is really quite simple. At some point in my previous pondering of the ladder and half-circle I had noted an apparent demarcation line between the half- circle and ladder. I folded the half-circle at a ninety degree angle to the ladder along this demarcation line and in the direction of the center disc. As I did this, the ladder was forced to bend downward at an angle, due to the half-circle meeting the center disc. All of this seemed like another wild goose chase until a resounding click occurred. In an instant *Stonehenge* had been deciphered (See Diagram 4C and Photo 15).

It was only moments later that I had the model spinning, and since we are talking about the bottom portion, let's continue with it (See Photos 17 and 18). Nothing could have prepared me for what occurred next. What was once the ladder had now become a transparent, perfectly formed energy field. Furthermore, the actual shape of the bottom of the machine was being revealed. It appeared that the middle portion was concave and contained an energy field that ran parallel to the concave bottom.

Up to this point in my travels through the crop circles, there was always a nagging doubt about the whole thing. After all, there was absolutely no one that I could turn to for confirmation. However, at the moment that this model began spinning and the ladder transformed into a beautiful, whirling energy field, instant confirmation occurred. I remember sitting there stunned at what I was seeing. It was an absolutely unbelievable moment as exhilaration and elation poured through my mind and body. I felt I was truly communicating with beings from across the galaxy.

The top portion of the model also contained its surprises (See Photos 16 and 17). Just as in *Barn Head*, the whirling antennae indicated an energy field that extended from the center shaft out to the edge of the top disc. In this case, the two spheres attached to the ends of the antennae created yet another energy formation just above them. In addition, the two eyebrows now formed a double sphere above the whirling spheres. Something was really happening along the vertical shaft. Exactly what, was slowly being revealed. I knew that it was just a matter of time before the answers would come rushing forth. With this thought in mind, I decided to take a look at another insectogram that very closely resembled this one.

Before we visit the third insectogram I would like to bring an interesting observation to your attention and particularly to any particle physicists who may be reading this material. Please return your attention to Photos 16 and 17. Look closely at the top double sphere being formed by the spinning double eyebrows. This is our initial encounter with this double sphere, however, it will reappear two more times within the crop circles addressed in this book. The

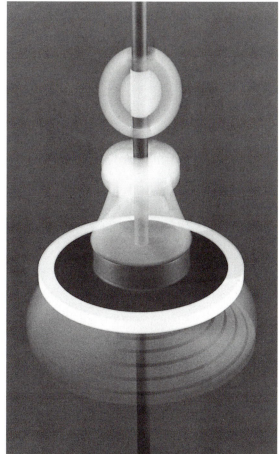

Photo No. 15: Model Stationary
(Bottom View)

Photo No. 16: Model Spinning
(Top View)

crop circle creators are continually repeating information for two primary reasons. First, they are confirming our correct analysis of previously deciphered crop circles and second, they are emphasizing important information. Coincidental with the preceding observations is that many facets to the puzzle created by the crop circles are revealed within a single crop circle formation. In the case of the double sphere, the creators of the crop circles are communicating the actual, physical structure of a particle that is the primary power source for the vehicle revealed within the crop circle formations.

STONEHENGE

Photo No. 17: Model Spinning
(Side View)

Photo No. 18: Model Spinning
(Bottom View)

THE THIRD INSECTOGRAM: LITCHFIELD
created in June, 1991

LITCHFIELD

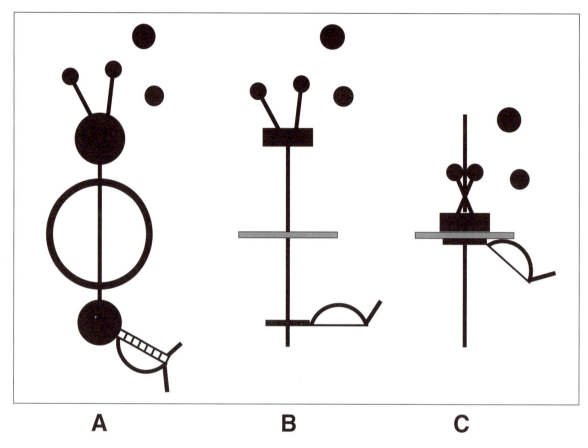

Diagram No. 5: Assembly

A) Diagram of the *Litchfield* crop circle as it appeared in the field.
B) The three discs have been rotated ninety degrees.
C) The two antennae have crossed each other due to the spheres attached to their ends. When this occurs, the two floating spheres move with their associated antenna to the position shown. Beneath the model, the arc portion of the ladder assembly rotates ninety degrees, forcing the ladder downward at a specific angle. The two extensions close until meeting each other, thus forming another specific angle.

THE THIRD INSECTOGRAM:
LITCHFIELD

The *Litchfield* insectogram is identical to the *Stonehenge* formation with two exceptions (See Diagram 5A). First, the floating eyebrows have been replaced by two floating spheres. Second, two extensions have been added to the ladder and half-circle.

Since I had just completed *Stonehenge*, the assemblage of this model was a snap (See Diagram 5A-C). To assemble the model, I duplicated my steps taken in assembling the *Stonehenge* model. First, the three discs were rotated ninety degrees as depicted in Diagram 5B. Second, the antennae were folded up against the vertical shaft and the floating spheres now traveled with the right antenna and ended up as you see them in Diagram 5C. The bottom of the model assembled identically to the *Stonehenge* model. As for the vertical extensions on the ladder and half-circle, I simply fiddled with them for a few minutes before a resounding click occurred. The two appendages simply bent inwards towards each other and joined very nicely (See Diagram 5C and Photos 19, 20, & 21). The attached extensions now formed a right angle to the ladder. Again, I had no idea what this meant.

Upon spinning the model something totally unexpected happened (See Photo 22). The whirling floating spheres, in concert with the spheres attached to the top of the antennae, were indicating something quite different from anything that I had come across previously. The floating spheres were creating an energy field with its terminuses at the center shaft and the outer ring of the center disc, not the top disc. This observation focused my attention on the center disc that always contained an outer ring, while the top disc never did. Maybe this elusive energy field extended from the center shaft to the outer ring of the center disc. Perhaps the antennae in all three insectograms were pointing, not to the edge of the top disc, but to the outer ring of the center disc!

The bottom of the spinning model appeared identical to the *Stonehenge* spinning model with the exception of the two extensions. They now revealed a new aspect to the shape of the physical structure being revealed (See Photo 22). It was now obvious that the edge to the lower portion of the shape being revealed was at a right angle to the angled inner cone. I did not have a clue what all of this meant. I simply made note of the information, filing it away for future reference.

LITCHFIELD

Photo No. 19: Model Stationary
(Top View)

Photo No. 20: Model Stationary
(Side View)

LITCHFIELD

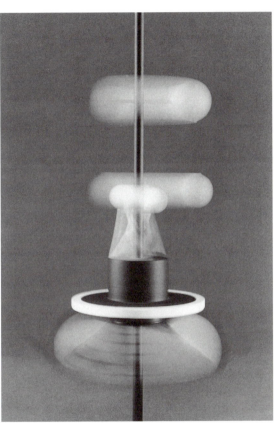

Photo No. 21: Model Stationary
(Bottom View)

Photo No. 22: Model Spinning
(Top & Side View)

LITCHFIELD

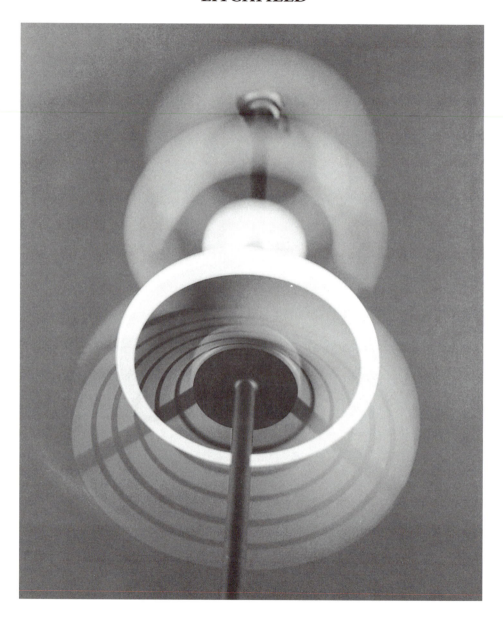

Photo No. 23: Model Spinning
(Bottom View)

CHAPTER FIVE

The Key Pictograms

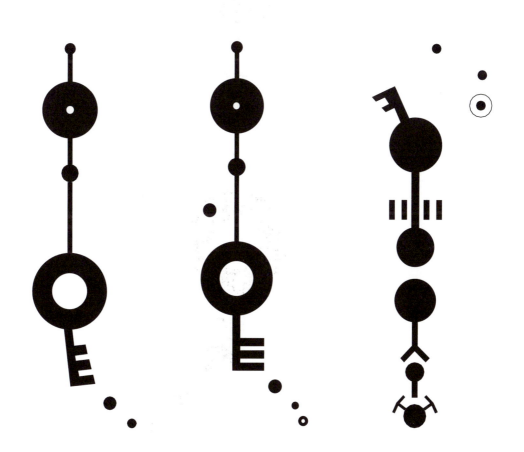

ALTON PRYORS
created July 19, 1991

KENNETS
created July 27, 1991

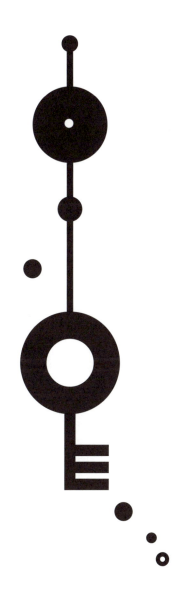

During the summer of 1990 and concurrent with the appearance of the insectograms, another type of pictogram was being created for the first time. These pictograms also contained their unique signature, namely, a formation within the crop circle resembling a key. Initially, these keys were crude in nature compared to later renderings. The English named these forerunners to the keys, claws, as that is what they resembled. I chose two of the key pictograms to decipher.

By this time I was on a merry chase within the crop circles and was savoring every crop circle and every discovery. I knew that I was on the trip of my life. I felt that I was also being introduced to the creators of the crop circles. Insights into their personalities and values were being revealed. I was fully aware that my experiences were paralleling those of both the trainers and the dolphins and orcas; only I was the dolphin or orca.

This inner reflection led me to another insight. To communicate on this level both parties must contain an inner peace as well as a genuine respect for their counterpart. If you have or ever do visit a dolphin or orca show, it will become immediately apparent to you that both parties involved do exhibit these qualities. I can assure you that it is an unbelievable high.

ALTON PRYORS/KENNETS

Two grandiose key pictograms appeared just one week apart during July of 1991. The first to appear was *Alton Pryors* on July 19, followed by the *Kennets* on July 27. The two formations were almost identical except for a difference in the keys and two additional spheres that the *Kennets* formation contained (See Diagram 6A, B). I built models of both crop circles and preferred the *Alton Pryors* model, to which I added the additional spheres from the *Kennets* pictogram. Diagram 6C indicates the compilation of these two pictograms. I concluded that this was the proper thing to do for a couple of reasons:

First, it is only logical to use all the information available. Second, the creators of the crop circles expended much effort to communicate complete and precise information. Evidently, one crop circle containing all of these spheres was considered too cluttered for their purposes. On the other hand, I found the two formations quite compatible.

Please note that the third sphere out from the key is another double sphere. Also note its relationship with the other spheres as indicated in the model at rest and spinning. Now, let's continue with the *Alton Pryors/Kennets* model.

ALTON PRYORS/KENNETS

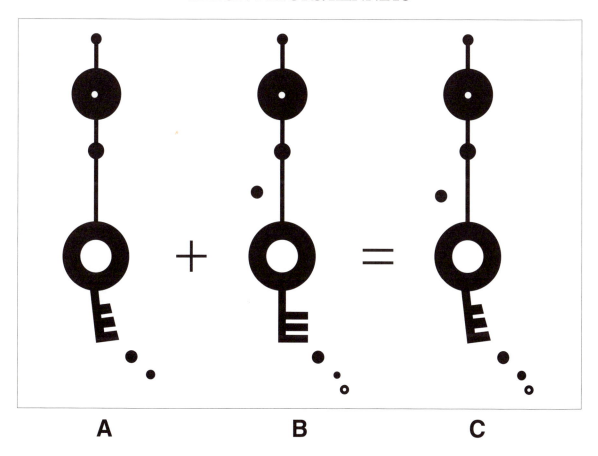

A   B   C

Diagram No. 6: Addition of *Alton Pryors and Kennets*

A) Diagram of the *Alton Pryors* crop circle as it appeared in the field.
B) Diagram of the *Kennets* crop circle as it appeared in the field.
C) The result of combining the *Alton Pryors* and *Kennets* formations.

Diagram 7 leads us through the decipherment of the crop circle. Diagram 7A depicts the *Alton Pryors/Kennets* formation that we just arrived at. Diagram 7B indicates that the two discs have been rotated ninety degrees. Notice that the key has simultaneously rotated ninety degrees and that the floating spheres have rotated with it. Diagram 7C indicates the movement of the upper disc downward until it meets the key that has moved inward and is now functioning as a spacer. The floating sphere located above the model remains at its original location.

It's amazing how one little paragraph can

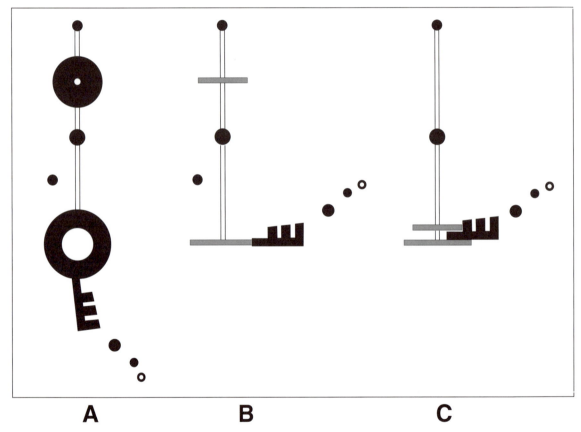

A　　　　　**B**　　　　　**C**

Diagram No. 7: Model Assembly

A) Diagram of the *Alton Pryors/Kennets* formation as depicted in Diagram 6C.
B) The two discs have been rotated ninety degrees.
C) The top disc has been moved inward until it reaches the key that has also moved inward and is forming the spacer.

contain a week's worth of skull drudgery. As you can see, this pictogram is unique in its decipherment. The crop circle creators spent a great deal of time dreaming up these diverse formations.

ALTON PRYORS/KENNETS

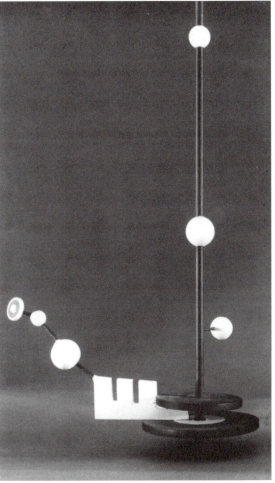

Photo No. 24: Model Stationary
(Top View)

Photo No. 25: Model Stationary
(Side View)

ALTON PRYORS/KENNETS

Photo No. 26: Model Spinning Vertical
(Top View)

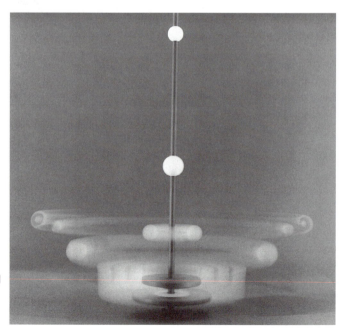

Photo No. 27: Model Spinning
(Side View)

Photo 26 is of the top of the model spinning. Notice that all three forks of the key now form the outer ring of the top disc. In other words, there are three distinct rings on the top disc, not just one. This will prove to be an important observation later on. Photo 27 is a side view of the model and indicates the relationship between the key and the spheres on the center shaft. The three spheres extending out from the key literally form a bowl about the center shaft. The key, with its three notches, is attracting spheres from the center shaft to it. Thus, the three floating spheres can be seen as in-transit from the center shaft to the key. This smacks of the negative/positive relationship exhibited by electromagnetism.

I can assure you that the information being communicated here does not involve either electricity or electromagnetism, but rather something very similar. The spheres indicated within the crop circles represent particles that exhibit the qualities of electromagnetism but do not contain an electrical charge. For our purposes, we will discuss them as relating to electromagnetism, since this is comprehensible to us. Let's continue under this pretext.

In a universal language, this is what the spinning model is communicating. It is becoming apparent that the center shaft represents a beam of positively charged particles that are being attracted to the negatively charged rings of the center disc. It is this flow of positively charged particles that is forming the energy field revealed by the antennae in the insectograms' spinning models. This energy field can now be interpreted to be akin to an electromagnetic field. Furthermore, the rings of the center disc definitely constitute the outer terminus of the energy field. Let's take a look at another key pictogram that will shed more light on this subject.

NEWTON-ST. LOWE
created in 1991

Original drawing by Richard Elen
From *Dowsing The Crop Circles*

NEWTON-ST. LOWE

To me, the *Newton-St. Lowe* formation is a mystery crop circle. All that I know about it is that it was created sometime during the summer of 1991. Remember, 1990 saw approximately a thousand crop circles appear in this area of England and the crop circle investigators were understandably overcome by this deluge. I discovered *Newton-St. Lowe* in my little yellow book, ***Dowsing The Crop Circles***, where it was presented in diagram form only. My other books did not even mention this one. As far as I am concerned, the dowsers saved this very important key pictogram from extinction.

The *Newton-St. Lowe* crop circle is similar to the *Alton Pryors/Kennets* formation. Both formations contain floating spheres and keys. Besides, a bonus accompanied this crop circle. It is a double pictogram. A double pictogram is one that is presented as two separate crop circles within a single formation. The English named these disconnected crop circles double pictograms.

When I attempted to decipher the crop circle, I immediately ran into problems. Initially, I couldn't figure out how the two sections of this double pictogram (top and bottom) integrated with each other (See Diagram 8A). Ultimately, I realized that the center and bottom discs were present in the top half of the formation while the top disc was completely missing. In Diagram 8B the center and bottom discs have been rotated ninety degrees. Notice that the key has also rotated ninety degrees and the floating spheres have remained with it. The bottom half of the formation is exactly as it appears. Very tricky!

The final assembly of the model, as depicted in Diagram 8C, proved to be a real brain teaser. The center and bottom discs, along with the spacers, came together easily, but where the key fit in was a mystery. Finally, I simply rotated the key ninety degrees along with the floating spheres. I then moved the key inward along the underside of the center disc until the inner key contacted the bottom disc. The inside fork of the key now rested perfectly against the bottom disc and there was a discernible click when this occurred. The floating spheres again moved with the key during its inward travel and ended up as you see them in Diagram 8C. This seemed very strange until I spun the model and discovered what I had created.

As I mentioned earlier, the lower half of the formation is exactly what it indicates. In other words, nothing has to be done to it. I simply cut it out and mounted it on the vertical shaft below the bottom disc. You can see this in Photo 28. I now had a complete model of the crop circle and only needed to spin it to discover the information being communicated. By this time, the initial spinning of a model had become the reward for all the effort expended in creating it. This was the frosting on the cake, and I had come to savor these moments of

NEWTON-ST. LOWE

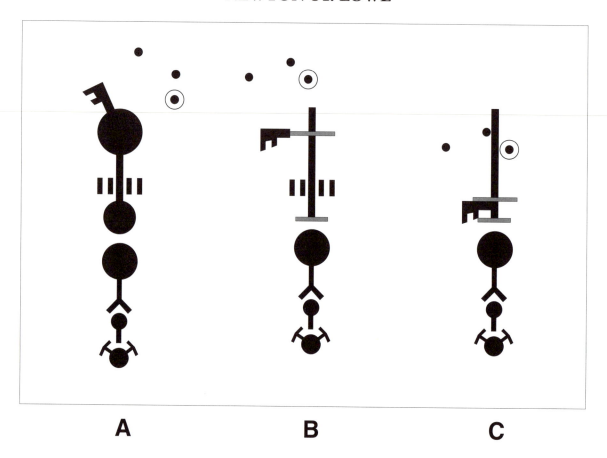

A   B   C

Diagram No. 8: *Newton-St.Lowe*

A) Diagram of the *Newton-St.Lowe* crop circle as it appeared in the field.
B) The two disks in the top portion of the formation have been rotated ninety degrees. When the center disc rotated ninety degrees, so did the key. The floating spheres followed the key. The bottom portion of the formation remains as it is.
C) The top disc has been moved down until it meets the vertical spacers. The spacers are not shown because they would become confused with the key. The key has been moved inward until the fork position touches the bottom disc.

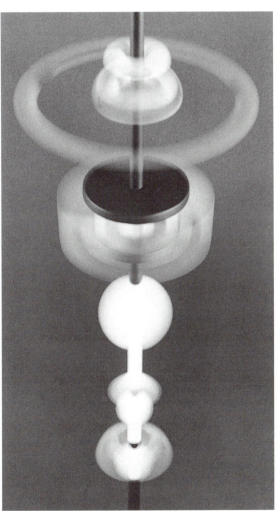

Photo No. 28: Model Stationary
(Top/Side View)

Photo No. 29: Model Spinning
(Top View)

NEWTON - ST. LOWE

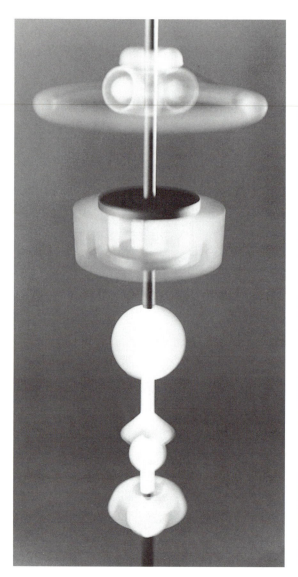

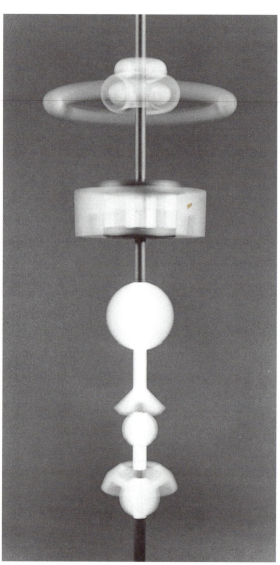

Photo No. 30: Model Spinning
(Top/Side View)

Photo No. 31: Model Spinning
(Side View)

instant knowledge and amazement.

The frosting provided by the spinning *Newton-St.Lowe* model was both novel and conclusive. In Photos 29, 30, and 31, you can see the dramatic formations created by the spinning model. Notice that the upper portion of the key is forming the outer ring of the center disc. This outer ring is being revealed to be an active participant with the whirling floating spheres above it. The spheres can be seen as in transit from the center shaft to the active outer ring of the center disc. You are probably asking yourself why only the outer ring is indicated as being active when we just saw three rings active in the *Alton Pryors/Kennets* model. Rest assured that both crop circles are correct and verification is forthcoming shortly. For now, let's continue with this model.

Again, the floating double sphere is present. In Photos 29, 30, and 31 we are offered another view of this all-important particle. The crop circle creators presented this particle to give us a clue as to its identity. They also used it for a second method of communication. Consider that we first encountered it in the *Stonehenge* model where it was incorporated within the vertical shaft. The next time that it appeared was in the *Alton Pryors/Kennets* model, where it was the third sphere out from the key. Now we see it departing the vertical shaft on its way to the outer ring of the center disc. The crop circle creators intentionally tagged this sphere in three different crop circles to indicate the path that all the particles are taking. Definite communi-

cation is taking place here to tell us that the ringed sphere is traveling from the vertical beam to the key. Again, we are offered verification of the terminuses of the electromagnetic field.

The bottom of the spinning model is revealing something that we have never seen before. Notice that the entire formation has now become both three-dimensional and transparent. What we are witnessing is a tremendous explosion of energy being emitted from the center of the bottom disc. This is in direct contrast to the slender beam emanating from the top of the model. This explosion of energy is composed of none other than our tagged, double sphere particle. Look closely at both formations located just below the large sphere in Photos 29, 30 and 31. Both of these formations are identical to the double spheres located at the top of the model. If you would place yourself mentally beneath the lowest sphere in the formation, you will see that it is identical to the rotating double spheres above the model. The crop circle creators are telling us that this one particle is used to power the entire ship. Therefore, it is important to study these photographs closely.

Newton-St.Lowe has verified our observations pertaining to the top of the model while offering us new information concerning the bottom portion. Let's take a look at another closely related crop circle that dovetails nicely with this one.

DOUBLE PICTOGRAM: THE GALLOPS
created August 4, 1990

A STAND ALONE DOUBLE PICTOGRAM
THE GALLOPS

This double pictogram is unique in both its presentation and its majestic beauty. In my opinion, this formation is the most beautiful of all the crop circles. It is similar to the *Newton-St. Lowe* pictogram, and the two formations complement each other.

Initially, I thought that this formation would be easy to decipher. Again I was wrong and ended up making two models before getting it right. Diagram 9 indicates the decipherment of *The Gallops* formation. At first glance it appeared that all three discs were present; however, on further inspection I realized that only the top and center discs were. In Diagram 9B the two discs have been rotated ninety degrees and the spacers have rotated to their upright positions. Notice that the two arcs at the top of the formation rotate with the top disc since they are floaters. The rest of the formation remains just as it is depicted. Diagram 9C indicates the movement of the top disc downward until it reaches the spacers. The model is now complete and can be viewed in Photo 32.

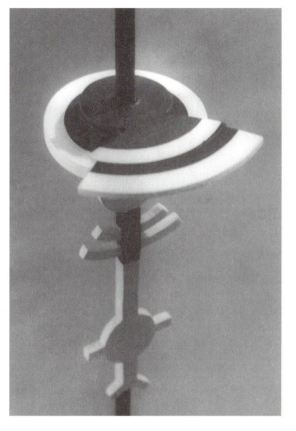

Photo No. 32: Model Stationary
(Top view)

THE GALLOPS

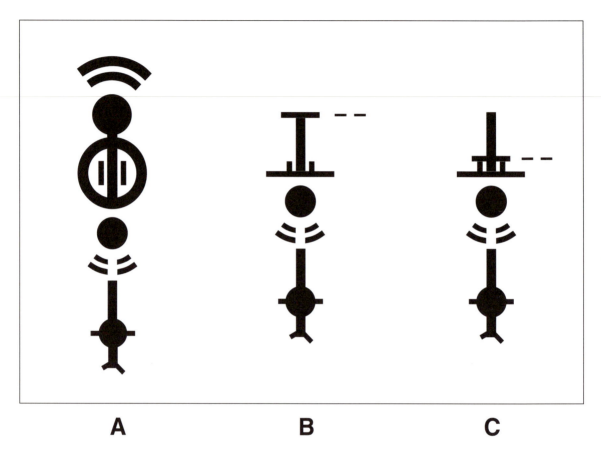

A   B   C

Diagram No. 9: Assembly of *The Gallops*

A) Diagram of *The Gallops* crop circle as it appeared in the field.

B) The two disks have been rotated ninety degrees. The spacers have also been rotated ninety degrees to their upright position. The floating arcs follow the top disc in its rotation as they constitute floaters. The bottom portion remains untouched.

C) The top disc moves downward until it meets the spacers.

THE GALLOPS

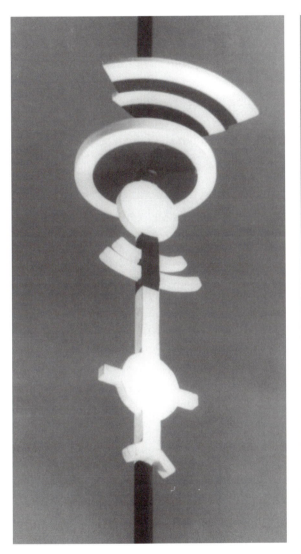

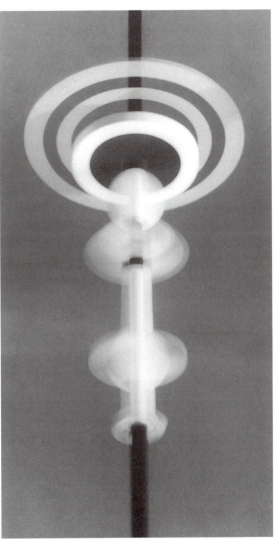

Photo No. 33: Model Stationary
(Bottom View)

Photo No. 34: Model Spinning
(Bottom View)

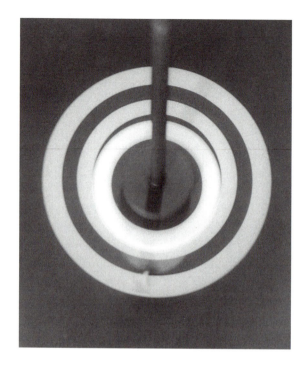

Photo No. 35: Model Spinning
(Top View)

When the model is spun, the twin-arcs extending out from the top disc form a transparent energy field that hovers over the outer ring and extends beyond it (See Photos 34, 35). Again, we have verification of a previous observation that one terminus of the energy field above the machine is the outer ring of the center disc.

The lower portion of the spinning model indicates a relationship between the explosive charges of energy being emitted from the bottom of the center disc and the outer ring of the center disc (See Photos 34, 35). This is indicated by the rotating twin-arcs and the energy field extending out from the center disc. Here we see the particles emitted from beneath the model being attracted to the outer ring.

To further understand the information being conveyed through the crop circles will require a little more than simply deciphering additional crop circles. It is my responsibility not only to explain the crop circles to you, but to do this as easily as possible. Our progress has been steady and a great deal has been learned about how the crop circles are deciphered and of the knowledge within them. However, I feel that we have reached an impasse and I do not want to confuse you by wandering around within the crop circles. To cut through the maze and enable you to understand the knowledge hidden within the crop circles, I am going to introduce you to another dimension of the phenomenon. This dimension is composed of a series of crop circles that are quite different from those we looked at previously. They are very special formations that reveal the actual shape of the machine. Once we have the machine, it will be much easier for you to understand the information being communicated.

CHAPTER SIX

The Ship

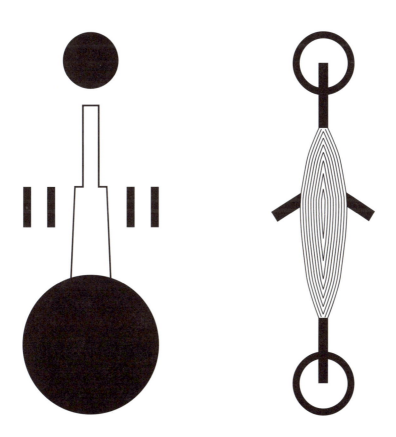

The crop circles we are about to decipher are, like the others, cumulative in nature. Information must be added from various circles to gain a complete picture of the message. The message, I have come to realize, is about the design of a saucer. We call them UFOs. Through the crop circles, their operators are inviting us to join them in greater knowledge of space travel. They are challenging us to put the pieces of the puzzle together, to work through the maze, and to see how it is done.

It has not been easy for me to decipher the various formations, and sometimes I simply have to ask you to trust that I know what I am talking about. I cannot stop to explain why I reach a certain conclusion as I discuss each crop circle. To do so would require a book the size of an encyclopedia and we would both get lost in a mountain of words. The repetition alone would bore us to death. Besides, with a little patience you will find that verification of my conclusions follows rather rapidly. Continue to keep an open mind, relax, and enjoy the revelation of extraterrestrial technology.

BISHOP CANNINGS ONE
created May 19, 1990

During the months of May and June of 1990, a small number of crop circles appeared in an area of England called Bishop Cannings. These crop circles were literally circles that contained numerous concentric and non-concentric circles. Diagram 10 is of one of these crop circles.

On May 27, 1990, a second photo was taken of this formation (See Diagram 12 on page 74). This photo revealed that an additional circle had been added between the two outermost circles (circle (E) added). This addition of another feature to an existing crop circle is called an add-on by the English. The addition of this circle, or ring, was done for a very specific reason that we will discover shortly in our discussion of ascent in Chapter Seven.

In deciphering these circles, I made the outer circle's diameter six inches and designated a letter for each ring. All the crop circles in this chapter are drawn to a six-inch scale that is further subdivided into tenths of an inch.

This crop circle depicts a vertical view of the top of the ship. In other words, we are looking down at the top of the ship. In the actual crop circle, the crops within the innermost circle (B) had been bent over, creating a pattern (shaded area). This center area within circle (B) is where the superstructure of the ship is located. All the outer rings are located on the outer disc. Now let's take a look at a new crop circle that will help us along our way.

BISHOP CANNINGS ONE

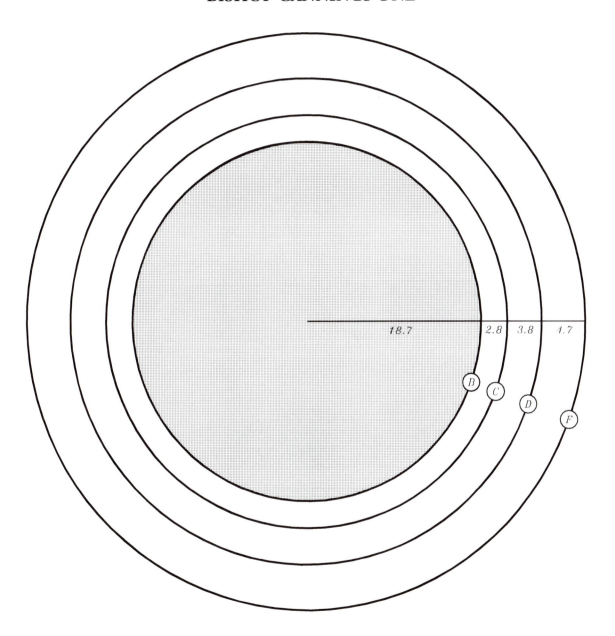

Diagram No. 10: Diagram of *Bishop Cannings One*

CHEESEFOOT HEAD OR FAT BOY

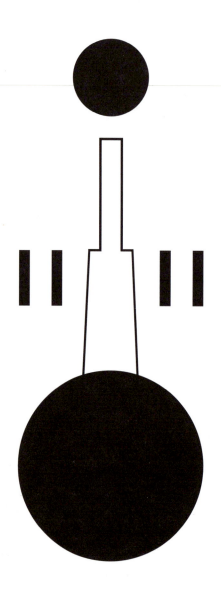

CHEESEFOOT HEAD OR FAT BOY

Cheesefoot Head was the first pictogram to appear during the 1990 crop circle season. I call it *Fat Boy* for reasons that you will soon discover. The crop circle initially appeared easy to decipher, but then proved to be very tricky.

Please refer to Diagram 11 as we decipher the crop circle and assemble the model. The formation contains only the top and center discs. The top, smaller disc, rotates ninety degrees and slides onto the cylindrical shaft until it reaches a lip (See Diagram 11A, B, C). The center, larger disc also rotates ninety degrees and slides onto the conical shaft until it contacts the spacers. Notice that in order for the large disc to slide onto the conical shaft, a hole must be cut in its center that is the same size as the lowest point on the conical shaft. Therefore, when the disc is slid up the shaft it will not fit snugly any longer, as its hole is much too large. However, it can still be attached to the spacers as depicted in Diagram 11C.

The formation was designed in this manner for a very clever reason. First, the gap existing between the top of the center disc and the conical shaft will be covered up by the top disc (See Diagram 11D & Photo 36). Second, and here is the reason for the whole puzzle, the gap between the conical shaft and the bottom of the large disc is revealed (See Diagram 11E & Photo 38). This thin ring indicates the presence of the bottom disc. Remember my earlier statement, that the bottom disc was not present in the diagram. Now, as the model is assembled, the bottom disc appears and is seen to be flush with the bottom of the center disc, just as it was in the *Alton Barnes* and insectogram models. Furthermore, we see the conical shaft originating from within the center disc and extending out of the flush bottom disc. This is very important information for future reference.

When we were addressing the *Alton Barnes* crop circle, I mentioned that it was the most important of all the crop circles. One of the main reasons for that statement was because the *Alton Barnes* model indicated all three discs and their relationship to each other. I also asked you to trust me in my determination of the top and bottom of the *Alton Barnes* model. This is one validation of that statement.

Now, let's return to the model of *Fat Boy* as seen in photos 36, 37, and 38. It should be quite obvious to you why I nicknamed it *Fat Boy,* as the center disc is very wide. Notice that the model is lacking a center shaft on which to spin. What is going on here? The answer lies in the realization that *Fat Boy* was never meant to be spun. Its sole purpose is to convey a very important piece of information. That information is the ratio between the diameter of the top disc, or the center disc, and the distance between them. This ratio enables us to determine the height of the top disc above the center disc for any given diameter of the center or top discs. Let's just simply do it and you will see what I am talking about.

CHEESEFOOT HEAD OR FAT BOY

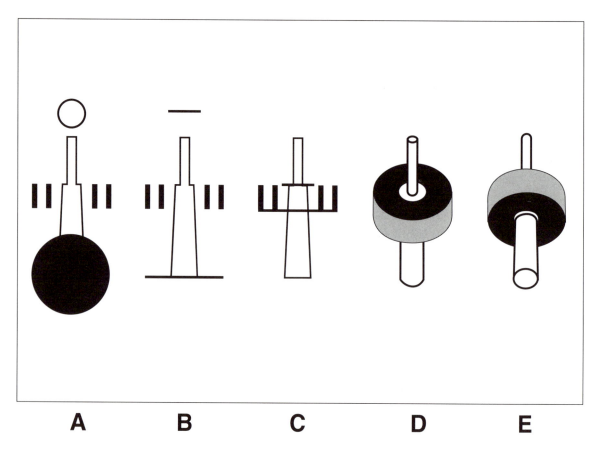

Diagram No. 11: Model Assembly

A) Diagram of the *Cheesefoot Head* crop circle as it appeared in the field.
B) The two discs have been rotated ninety degrees.
C) The two discs have been moved inward until reaching the vertical spacers.
D) The model has been rotated inward to allow you a view of its top.
E) The model has been rotated away to allow you a view of its bottom.

CHEESEFOOT HEAD OR FAT BOY

Photo No. 36: Top View of Model

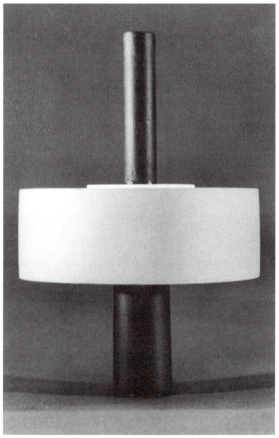

Photo No. 37: Side View of Model

CHEESEFOOT HEAD OR FAT BOY

Photo No. 38: Bottom View of Model

ADDITION

I'd like you to take another look at Diagram 10 on page 67, which is of the *Bishop Cannings One* crop circle. Notice that the inner circle of this diagram has been designated circle (B) and is shaded. This is the area where the crops have been bent and designates the location of the superstructure of the ship. Therefore, the top of the ship must be contained within this area. *Fat Boy* supplies us with the diameter of the top disc that is located within this area. That diameter is 26.2 tenths of an inch and constitutes circle (A) in Diagram 12.

Now let's take Diagram 12 and chop it in half, as depicted in Diagram 13. We already know that circle (A) designates the circumference of the top disc, which is also the top of the ship. By referencing *Fat Boy,* we can take our ratio between the thickness of the center disc to the diameter of either the top or center discs and acquire a distance between these two discs.

This distance for a six-inch diameter outer circumference is 21 tenths of an inch.

Two vertical lines of this length can be drawn from the two points (A) in Diagram 13. A horizontal line connecting these two points can be drawn. This line depicts the top disc. We now have the beginnings of a horizontal view of the ship.

Before we leave this diagram, there are a couple of additional vertical lines that can be added. We know that the shaded area within ring (B) indicates the location of the superstructure of the ship. Therefore, we can draw vertical lines at these two points (B). We also know that the outer edge of the ship is indicated by points (F). Therefore, we can add these two vertical lines. All the information that *Fat Boy* contains has now been extracted from it. To continue we will require the help of a whale.

ADDITION

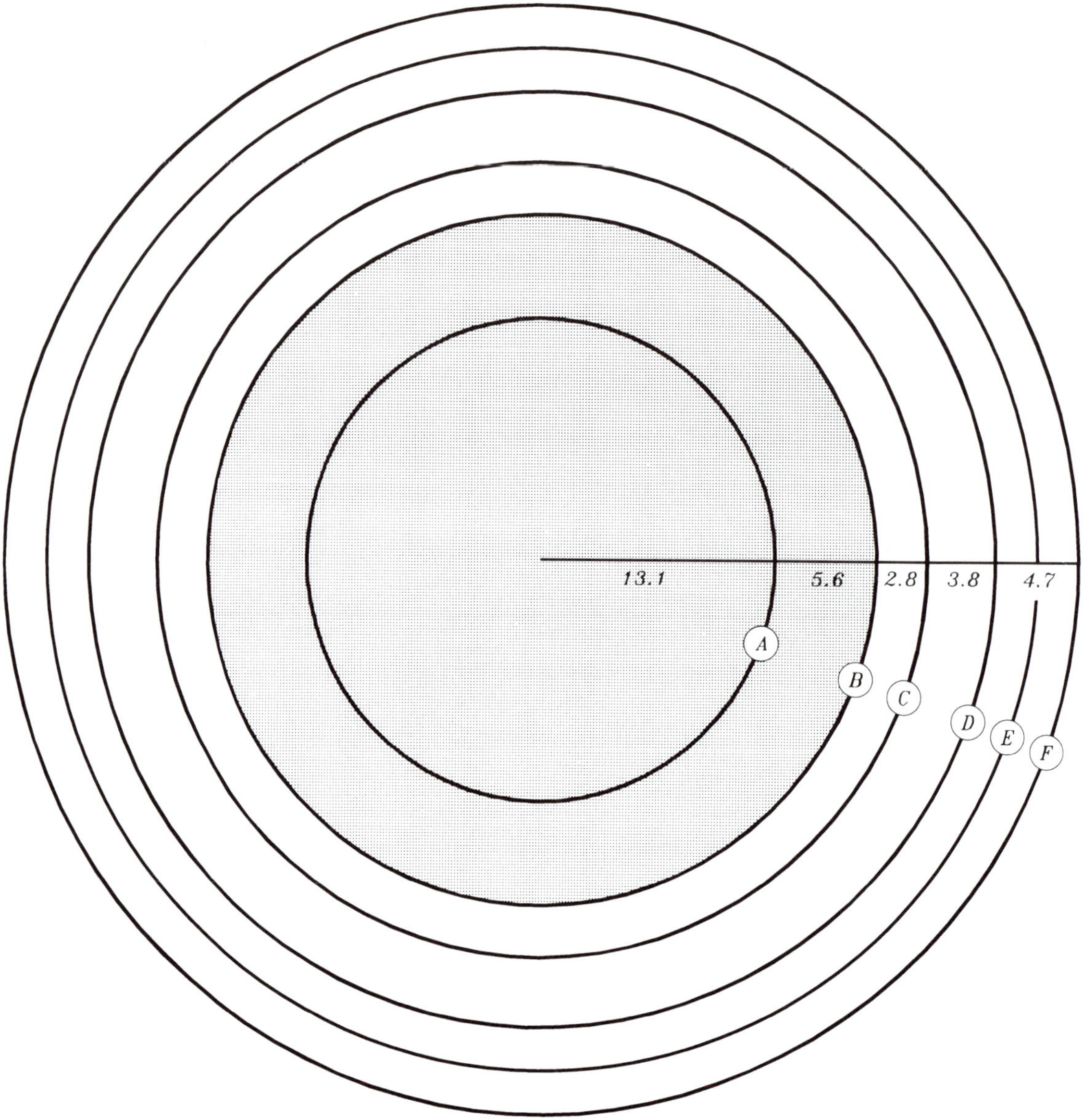

13.1   5.6   2.8 3.8   4.7

A
B
C
D
E
F

Diagram No. 12: Addition of top disc diameter to Diagram 11

ADDITION

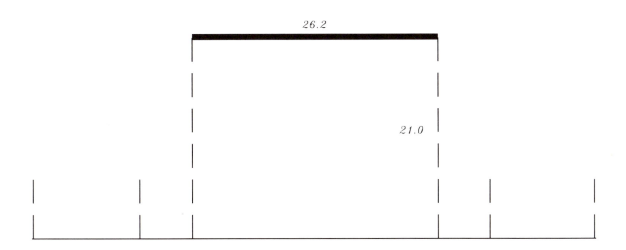

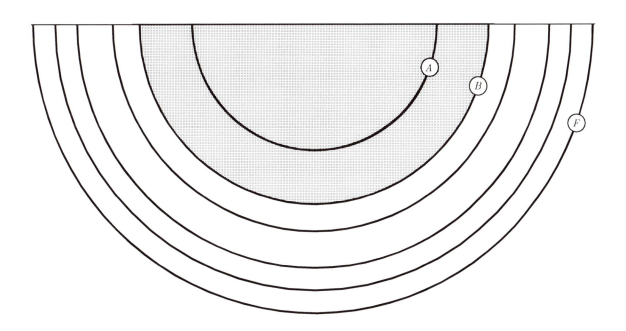

Diagram No. 13: Vertical height added to Diagram 12

THE FIRS FARM WHALE
created July 30, 1991

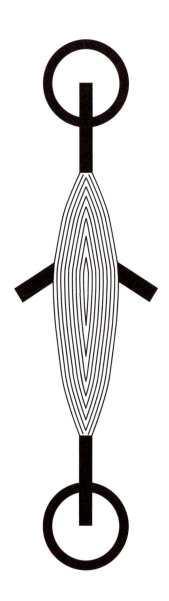

THE FIRS FARM WHALE

There were many whales created during the summer of 1991. Some were duplicates while others were one of a kind. I believe that so many were created because the crop circle makers were never satisfied with the formations. Many of the whales were not symmetrical or their fins were at different angles or lengths. Finally, beautiful, symmetric whales appeared. It was one of these perfect whales that I selected to decipher. It was a good thing that I was picky about my whale as the formation contained a crucial ingredient to the design of the ship.

The whale pictogram is a snap to decipher. The two rings rotate ninety degrees and slip over the whale until they reach the fins. That's all there is to it. (See Diagram 14 and Photo 39). Please note in the diagram that the two rings are of unequal size, denoting the top and bottom rings.

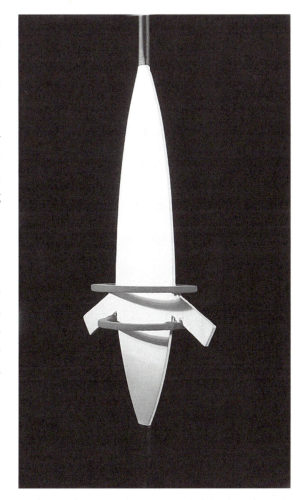

Photo No. 39: Model Stationary
(Side View)

THE FIRS FARM WHALE

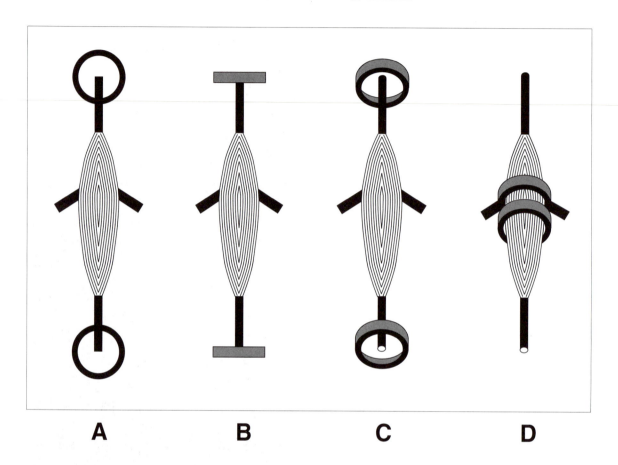

A   **B**   **C**   **D**

Diagram No. 14: Model Assembly

A) Diagram of the *Firs Farm Whale* formation as it appeared in the field.
B) The two rings have been rotated ninety degrees.
C) The model has been rotated away to allow you a better view.
D) The rings have been moved inward until they meet the fins.

THE FIRS FARM WHALE

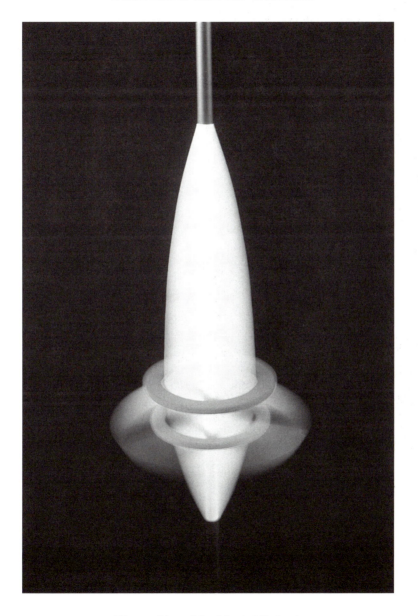

Photo No. 40: Model Spinning
(Top View)

Photo No. 41: Model Spinning
(Side View)

Take a look at Photos 39, 40, and 41. Notice that all three discs are present. The center disc is represented by the rotating fins. Also notice that the bottom disc is positioned right up under the rotating fins, or flush with the center disc. The relative size of the rings is again apparent in this model. The top ring is larger than the bottom ring and the center ring is larger than the top ring. All of these observations are verification of previous discoveries that we have made.

The crucial piece of information that the whale communicates is hidden within the fins. As we have just learned, the center disc is represented by the fins and the angle of these fins is thirty degrees. Therefore, we now know that the center disc of the ship slopes at a thirty degree angle! Let's apply this thirty degree angle to our horizontal diagram and see what happens.

ADDITION

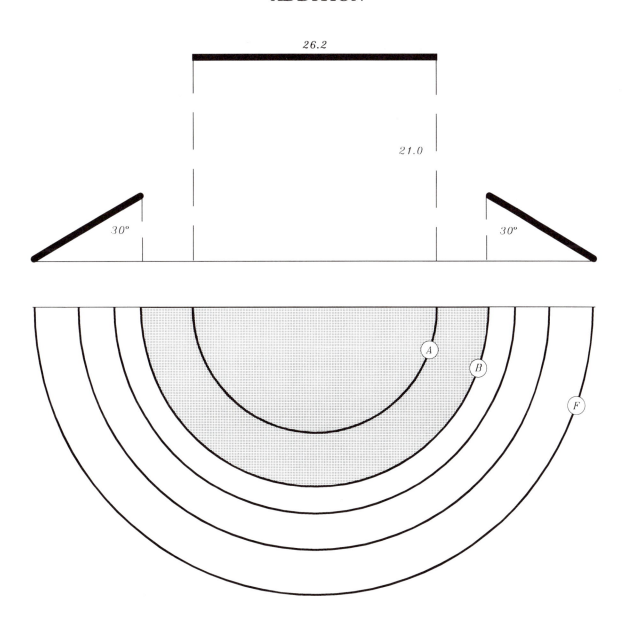

Diagram No. 15: With thirty degree angle added to Diagram 13

81

ADDITION

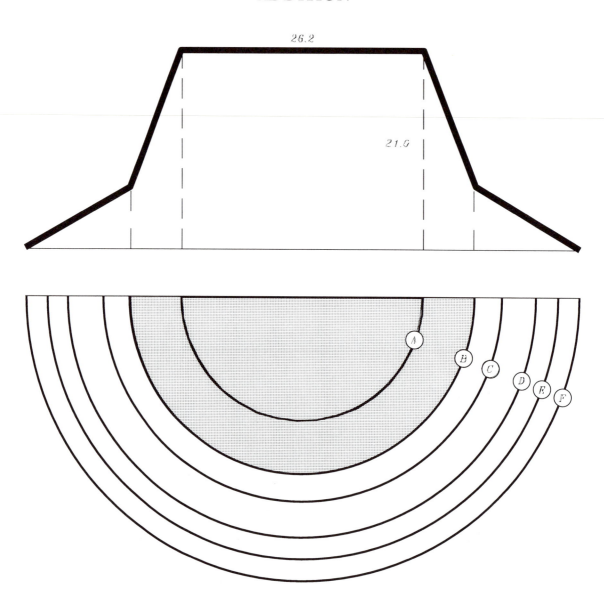

26.2

21.0

Diagram No. 16: Connecting A to B

DIAGRAM 15

As we look at Diagram 15, we know that the area between rings (B) and (F) is the area where the rings depicted in the *Bishop Cannings One* diagram are located, along with the whale's fins. Therefore, this area between points (B) and (F) is angled at thirty degrees. We can add this angle to our diagram by measuring a thirty degree angle from points (F). A line can then be drawn along this thirty degree angle from point (F) to point (B). We are now finished with this diagram.

DIAGRAM 16

Diagram 16 is very close to displaying a complete horizontal view of the top of the ship. However, a gap remains between points (A) and (B). Since both points are known, we can simply draw a line connecting them as depicted in Diagram 16. Now we have a complete horizontal view of the top of the ship.

THE BOTTOM OF THE SHIP

BISHOP CANNINGS TWO
created in early July, 1990

The *Bishop Cannings Two* crop circle is another circular crop circle that was created during the summer of 1990. Diagram 17 is of this crop circle. Again, just as in the *Bishop Cannings One* crop circle, the center crops have been bent to form a pattern. This patterned area has been shaded and indicates vertical structure beneath the ship. Notice that the narrow ring that abuts this inner circle closely resembles the bottom ring depicted in *Alton Barnes, The Whale* and *Fat Boy*. This is because it _is_ the bottom ring that circumscribes the bottom disc.

Just as I did in the *Bishop Cannings One* diagram, I have allocated a letter to each circle. As we have just discussed, the area within ring (A) contained crops that had been bent to form a pattern. This area within ring (A) has been shaded and indicates vertical structure beneath the ship. We also just arrived at the obvious conclusion that the narrow ring formed by rings (A) and (B) constitutes the bottom disc of the ship as depicted in both the *Alton Barnes* and *Whale* crop circle models. The remaining rings will reveal themselves in a few moments.

BISHOP CANNINGS TWO

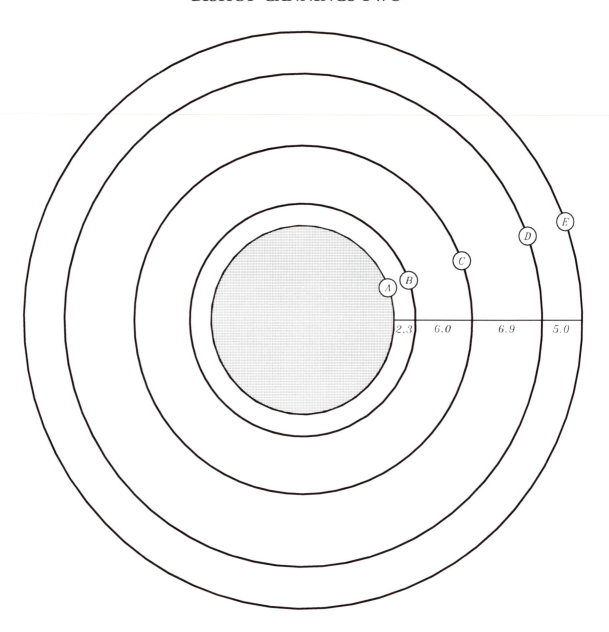

Diagram No. 17: *Bishop Cannings Two*

DIAGRAMS 18, 19, & 20

Take a look at Diagram 18. I have chopped Diagram 17 in half and drawn another horizontal line just below it to accommodate a horizontal view of the ship. We have just discussed the point that circle (B) inward constitutes the bottom disc and that this disc lies flush with the bottom of the ship. Therefore, the rest of the bottom of the ship must be at a thirty-degree angle as depicted in the whale. If you need to, refer to Photo 41 on page 80 to verify this observation.

In Diagram 18, I have marked off a horizontal line with its boundaries at the two points (B). I have then measured off a thirty degree angle from each point (B) and extended a line along this thirty degree angle.

There is still a gap in Diagram 18 that can be closed very easily (see Diagram 19). The whale's fins terminated in a ninety degree angle and this is exactly how the edge of the ship is shaped. This ninety-degree angle can be added to our diagram by measuring a right angle off the thirty degree angled line that intersects point (E). Notice how the width of the ninety degree angled outer edge matches perfectly with the outer ring (D-E). We now have a complete horizontal view of the bottom of the ship and all that remains is to combine the two halves.

Diagram 20 depicts the combining of the top and bottom horizontal views of the ship. Now that we have a scale drawing of the ship, a model can be made of it. Before we view the model, let's take a look at a few clues that the crop circle creators gave us along the way to validate the

shape of the ship.

1) The *Firs Farm Whale* formation told us that the outer disc was angled at thirty degrees.

2) It also told us that the edge of the ship angled at ninety degrees from the top and bottom of the center disc as well as indicating the location of the three discs.

3) The *Litchfield* insectogram also indicated the ninety degree edge to the ship.

4) Both the second and third spinning, insectogram models, *Stonehenge* and *Litchfield*, related the shape of the bottom of the ship in dramatic fashion.

5) The *Alton Barnes* model indicated the relationship, both in size and location, of the three discs.

6) Along with this, we now see how the bottom disc lies flush with the bottom of the center disc.

7) *Fat Boy* told us a great deal about the location of the three discs. The model came very close to giving us a picture of the entire ship. From it, the actual shape could be carved out.

It should be obvious to you by now that the crop circle creators were giving us clues all along the way. You might say that they were creating a little path for us to follow. The amazing point about the entire puzzle is that it doesn't matter where you enter the path or what clues you pick up along the way, you will always arrive at the same conclusion every time. There are still many more clues out there that we have not yet discussed. As we discover them, we will obtain a complete picture of how the ship operates.

ADDITION

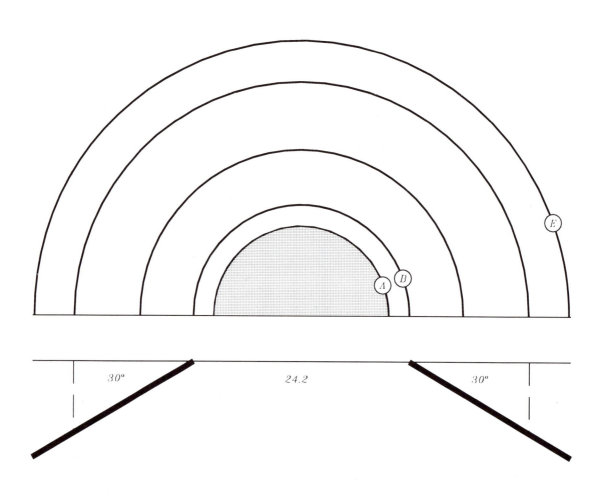

Diagram No. 18: *Bishop Cannings Two* (horizontal)

ADDITION

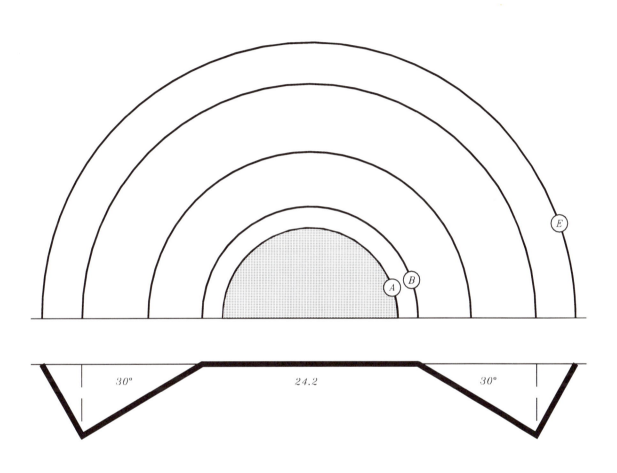

Diagram No. 19: Diagram 18 with ninety degree angle added

ADDITION

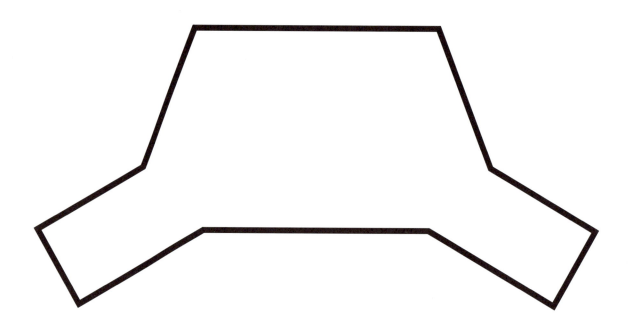

Diagram No. 20: Combining Diagrams 16 & 19

Photo No. 42: (Side View)

THE MODEL

All of this deciphering has been way too much work not to have a reward. Photos 42, 43 and 44 are of a scale model of the ship. This model was made from the plans that we just extrapolated from the crop circles.

The crop circle creators offer us quite a bit more than simply a scale model of the ship. They also explain its operation. To obtain this knowledge will require us to return to the crop circles. From here on out we will essentially be discussing the various functions of the ship and their related systems. For instance, we will discuss *ascent, descent, lateral motion, angular motion, stabilization,* and *power plant.* This approach will enable us to cut through the maze in which the crop circles are nestled while providing us with additional organization.

I believe that it would also benefit us if we could visit the actual ship. This can be accomplished rather easily by simply creating it. Let's take the six-inch diameter scale model and mentally increase its size 120 times, creating a sixty-foot diameter starship. For convenience sake, let's park the ship right outside the back door. Now we can take a short field trip anytime we desire to obtain a little hands on experience. All it takes is a little visualization and an open mind.

THE MODEL

Photo No. 43: (Top View)

Photo No. 44: (Bottom View)

CHAPTER SEVEN

Ascent

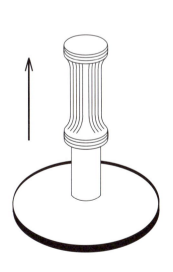

As we observed the crop circle models spinning, we arrived at a number of observations that can be carried over to the scale model. As I mention each of these, notice that they have been transferred to the model ship (See Diagram 21). First, we know that rings (B) through (F) in Diagram 12 (page 74), are all located on the angled outer rim of the ship. Second, we know that an outer ring located at the perimeter of the center disc comprises one terminus of an energy field. Third, there is a vertical beam that emanates from the center of the top disc.

Both the insectogram and key pictograms related to us that an energy field exists above the ship that extends from the vertical beam to the outer ring of the center disc. For purely discussion purposes, I will assign a positive charge to the particles that compose the vertical beam and a negative charge to the outer ring of the ship. The energy field now becomes an electromagnetic field extending from the vertical beam to the outer ring of the ship. In order for this field to exist, the material covering the ship must be capable of blocking an electromagnetic field. Otherwise, the negatively charged outer ring would be attracted to the positively charged particles within the ship, thus eliminating the field that we know exists. All the components required for ascension are now present. Let's take our first field trip to the ship to understand how this occurs.

As we sit at the ship's controls, our first action would be to energize the power source. Next we would activate the vertical beam gun and energize the outer ring. At this point we would have a beam of positively charged particles emanating from the beam gun. The outer ring would have a negative charge. As we increase power to both components, their charges would become stronger and stronger until an electromagnetic field is established between the two. As additional power is added, a threshold will be crossed and the ship will rise. The reason for this is something that we have all seen many times in photographs and drawings of UFOs. If you think about it, every saucer-shaped UFO always has the same basic shape to its top side. This universal shape is a fundamental requirement of the ship's operation. Once you see it, the obvious becomes overwhelming.

Notice in Diagram 22 that the only positively charged particles that the negatively charged outer ring can see are those within that portion of the vertical beam located well above the ship. This is due to the shape of the ship. Since the outer ring is attracted to a point on the vertical beam above the ship, the ship will rise as the outer ring attempts to move towards the elevated positive charge. There is a simple analogy that explains this very well.

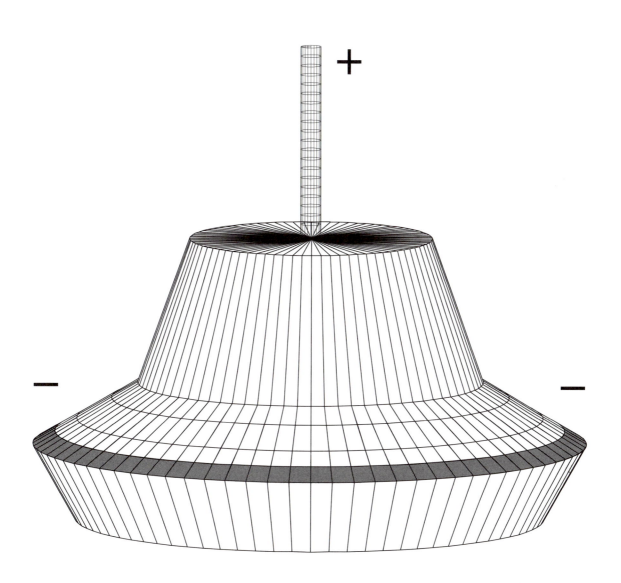

Diagram No. 21:
Ship with positively charged vertical beam and negatively charged outer ring

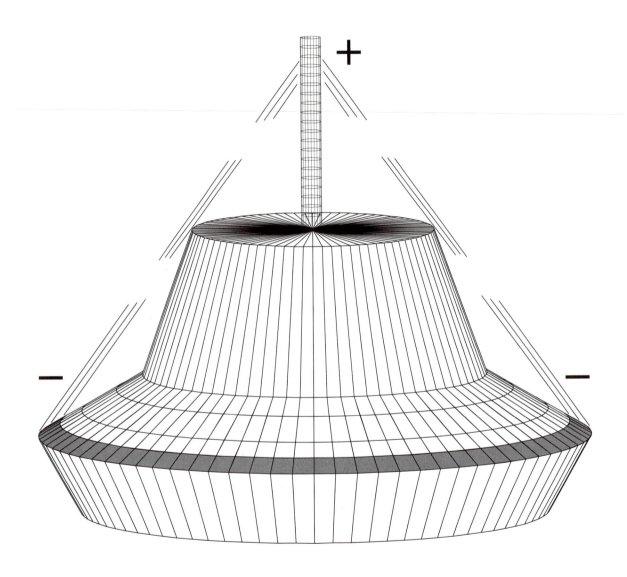

Diagram No. 22: Diagram 21 with the addition of the energy field in place

TWO RINGS OF MAGNETS

Diagram 23 illustrates two rings. The top ring is elevated and held in place by a bracket. A number of bar magnets have been attached to it with all of their positive ends facing downward. The lower, negatively charged ring is held in place by two retaining clamps.

In Diagram 24 the lower, negatively charged, ring's retaining clamps have been released. The lower ring has risen and attached itself to the positively charged ends of the elevated magnets. Opposites attract.

If these two rings are transferred to the ship, the negatively charged lower ring becomes the negatively charged outer ring of the ship. The upper ring becomes the positively charged vertical beam. Since the only portion of the vertical beam that the negatively charged ring can see is well above the ship, the ship will ascend towards it but never catch it. Obviously the outer ring is an integral part of the ship and the ship will ascend as the outer ring ascends. This is pretty simple stuff with awesome results.

A LITTLE PROBLEM

There is an innate problem with this scenario that I did not recognize until I noticed it in a number of crop circles. Here is the problem. Immediately after the electromagnetic field is established the ship would automatically ascend at a high rate of acceleration. This vertical acceleration would be akin to starting up your automobile and having it instantaneously accelerate to sixty miles per hour. In other words, in its present state the ship has only two speeds, stationary and extremely fast. This is due to the sudden establishment of such a powerful electromagnetic field.

Take another look at Diagram 22 and notice the distance this field spans. It extends from the outer ring of the center disc all the way to a point on the vertical beam high above the ship. The amount of energy required to establish such a large field would exceed that required to create ascension. Thus, this initial field would be so powerful that the ship would accelerate very rapidly, as if it had been shot out of a cannon. The solution to the problem lies within four crop circles, one of which we have already deciphered.

TWO RINGS

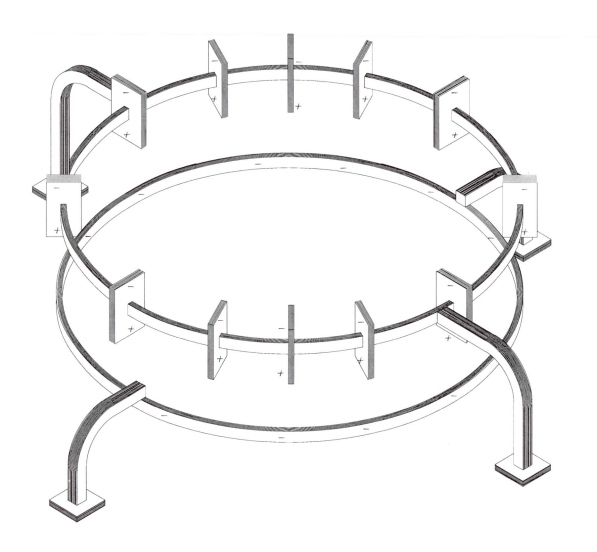

Diagram No. 23: Two rings of magnets apart

TWO RINGS

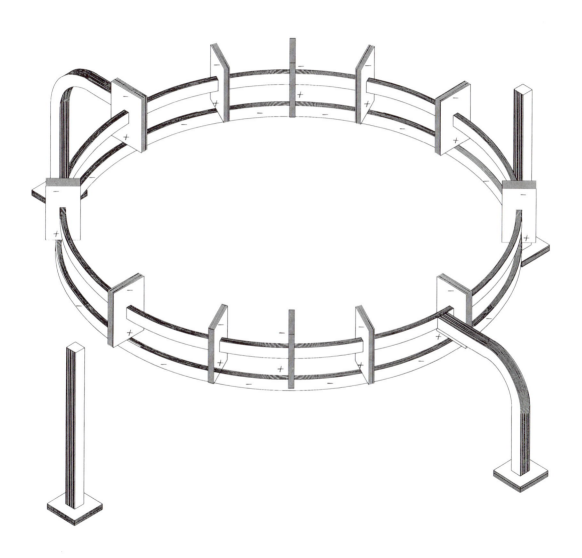

Diagram No. 24: Two rings of magnets together

THE CAMBRIDGE PICTOGRAM
date of creation unknown

Diagram 25A is a drawing of the *Cambridge* pictogram. Diagram 25B indicates that the large disc has been rotated ninety degrees and now sits on top of the bent shaft. The object on top of the disc is the particle beam gun. It remains in the center of the disc as indicated.

Notice how the disc rotates when the bent arm of the shaft is turned. Now we focus our attention on the gun mount that has a hole in its center. If a round dowel is placed in this hole, the gun mount and gun would be capable of rotating from a horizontal position all the way to a vertical position. This attribute of the beam gun can be viewed in Diagram 25C. The crop circle creators were communicating to us that the beam gun is capable of rotating in both the horizontal and vertical axis. To understand the part that this twin-axis, rotating beam gun plays in ascension will require the help of two additional crop circles.

THE CAMBRIDGE PICTOGRAM

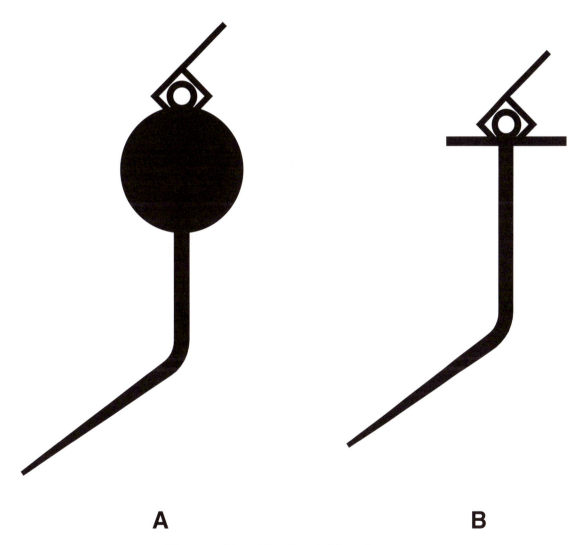

A   **B**

Diagram No. 25: *Cambridge* pictogram

A) Diagram of the *Cambridge* crop circle as it appeared in the field.
B) The disc has been rotated ninety degrees. The entire gun assembly located above the
   disc remains in its vertical position in the center of the disc.

THE CAMBRIDGE PICTOGRAM

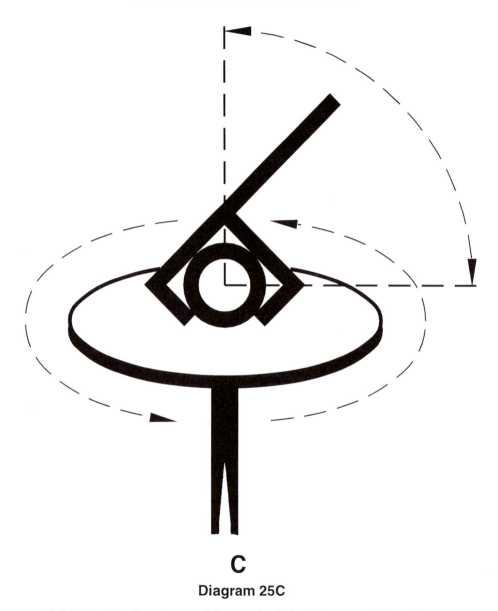

C

Diagram 25C

C) [See page 99] When the bent arm of the vertical shaft is rotated, the disc and gun assembly rotate horizontally. The gun is also capable of rotating in its vertical plane from a horizontal position to a vertical position while simultaneously rotating horizontally.

ETCHILHAMPTON
created in 1990

ETCHILHAMPTON

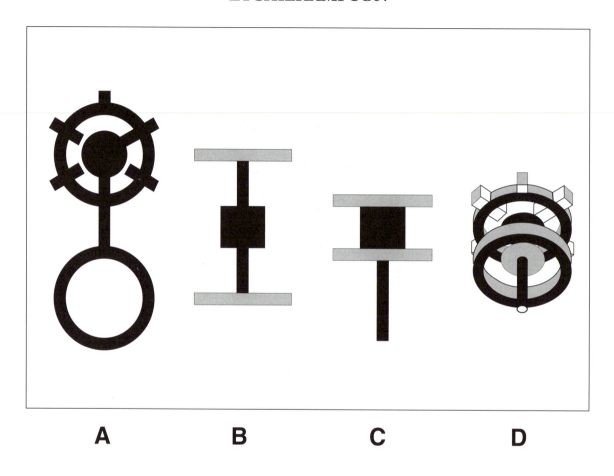

A   B   C   D

Diagram No. 26: Diagram of Formation

A) Diagram of the *Etchilhampton* crop circle as it appeared in the field.
B) The two discs have been rotated ninety degrees. The distance between the two discs in 26A becomes the spacer.
C) The two discs have been moved inward until they meet the spacer.
D) The model has been rotated to allow you a better view.

ETCHILHAMPTON
created in 1990

This crop circle is one of many dumbbell formations that appeared during the summer of 1990. Diagram 26A is a drawing of this crop circle, while Diagram 26B indicates that the two discs have been rotated ninety degrees. Notice that the spacer is indicated by the distance between the two discs. The upper and lower discs then slide together to form the model as depicted in Diagram 26C, D and Photo 45.

Photo 46 is of the model spinning. What we are seeing is the positively charged field created by the spinning particle beam gun while in its horizontal position. This is verification of the rotation of the beam gun to its horizontal position.

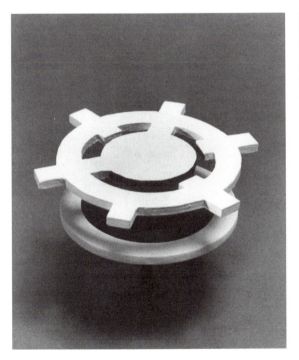

Photo No. 45: Model Stationary
(Top View)

Photo No. 46: Model Spinning
(Top View)

BARBURY CASTLE
created on July 17, 1991

The *Barbury Castle* pictogram is by far the most complex crop circle ever created. The only requirement to decipher the crop circle is the ability to view it three-dimensionally.

Diagram 27A is a drawing of the formation, while in Diagram 27B the entire formation has been tilted ninety degrees. Photo 48 is of the model derived from the diagram.

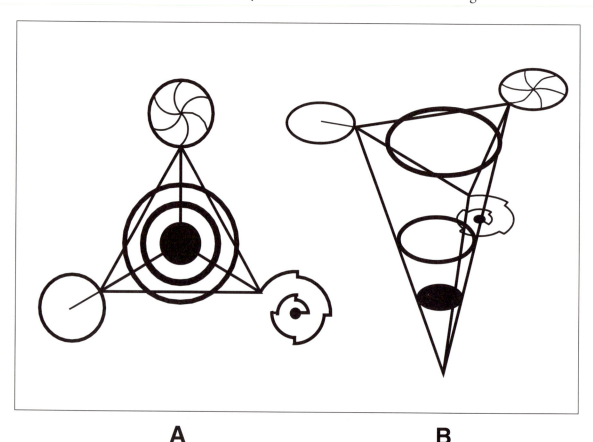

A　　　　　　　　　　**B**

Diagram No. 27: *Barbury Castle*

A) Diagram of the *Barbury Castle* crop circle as it appeared in the field.
B) The entire formation has been tilted ninety degrees to view its vertical position. Notice that nothing in the formation was required to rotate to decipher it.

BARBURY CASTLE

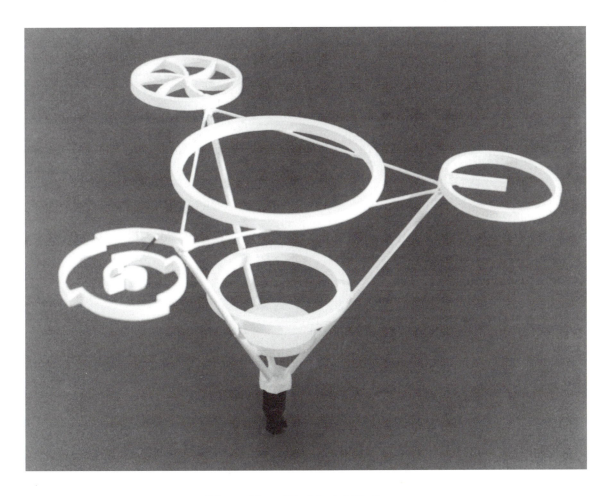

Photo No. 47: Model Stationary
(Top/Side View)

BARBURY CASTLE

Photo No. 48: Model Spinning
(Top View)

BARBURY CASTLE

Photo No. 49: Model Spinning (Side View)

When the model is spun, as seen in Photo 49, it depicts the beam gun firing at approximately a forty-five degree angle during its travel from either its horizontal or vertical position. Photo 48 offers a vertical view of the top of the ship with the angled beam gun firing. As you can see, the pattern created is quite dramatic.

The creators of this crop circle expended a lot of time and energy on this intricate formation to communicate a simple, straight forward function of the rotating beam gun. On the other hand, perhaps there is more here than meets the eye. We will revisit this pictogram during our discussion of the power plant. At any rate, it took one smart ET to dream this one up.

The *Cambridge, Etchilhampton,* and *Barbury Castle* pictograms have given us a double-axis, rotating particle beam gun and two of the formations it is capable of forming. To understand the part that this modified beam gun plays in controlled ascent, let's first mount it on top of the ship.

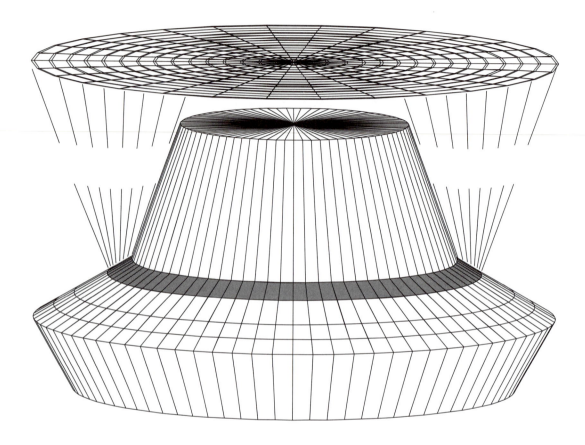

Diagram No. 28A: Diagram with inner ring activated

To understand controlled ascent, let's slip out the back door and into the ship. After cranking it up, our next action would be to initiate the creation of the electromagnetic field, just as we had done previously, only with a ripple. This ripple is comprised of an automatic procedure built into the ship's electronics and would go something like this (See Diagram 28A)

1) The beam gun would rotate to its horizontal position and create a horizontal, positively charged field just above the top of the ship.
2) The innermost ring would be negatively charged and an electromagnetic field established between it and the positive field just above it. Notice the length of the electromagnetic field formed here. It is much shorter than the original field, and therefore

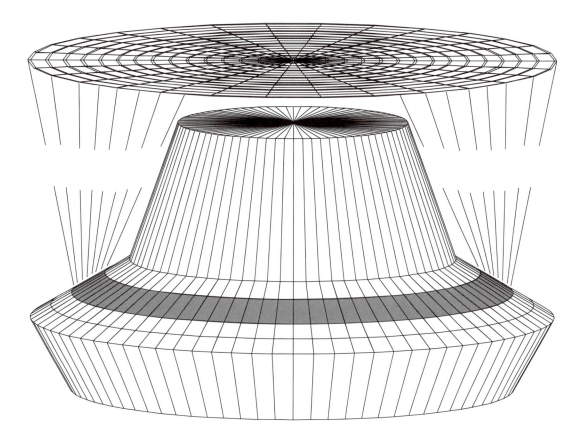

Diagram No. 28B: Diagram with second ring only activated

required much less energy to form it.
Let's continue.

Diagram 28B indicates that three things have occurred:

1) The innermost ring has become deactivated.
2) The second ring out has become activated.
3) The electromagnetic field has jumped to the second ring out.

Diagram 28C (Page 110) indicates that three things have occurred:

1) The second ring out has become deactivated.
2) The third ring out (D-F) has become activated.
3) The electromagnetic field has jumped to the third ring out.

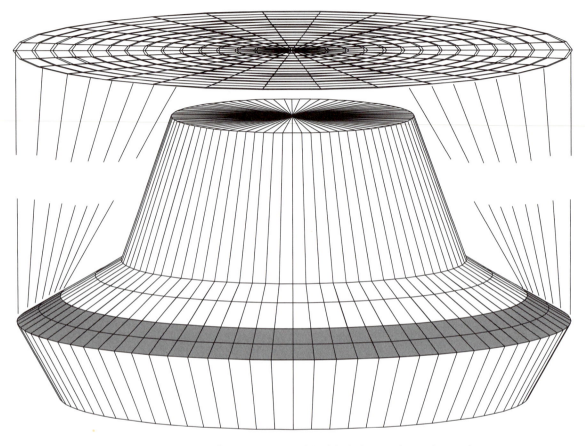

Diagram No. 28C: Diagram with third ring only activated

Diagram 28D indicates that two things have occurred:

1) The inner half of the third ring has become deactivated.

2) The electromagnetic field is now established with only the outer half of the third ring.

Diagram 29 (Page 112) is a drawing of the *Bishop Cannings One* crop circle discussed in Chapter Six. As mentioned, there was a time sequence built into this crop circle—an add-on as the British called it. The formation appeared on May 19, 1990, minus ring (E). On May 27, 1990, ring (E) was added. Through this delay the crop circle creators were telling us to ripple the rings outward in a wavelike motion. Then, once the outermost ring (D-F) is energized and the field established, its inner half (D-E) is de-energized. This process leaves us with just ring (E-F) energized. Trust me!

110

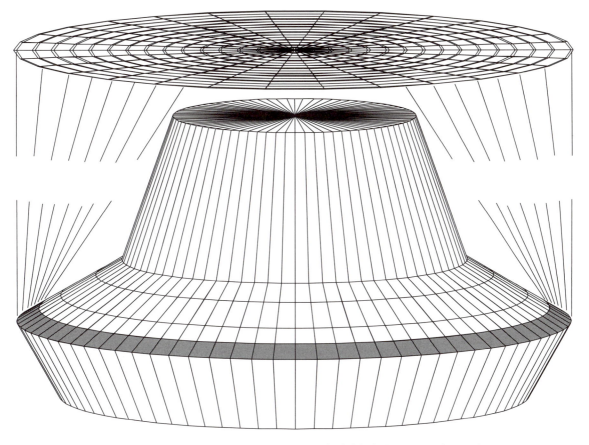

Diagram No. 28D: Diagram with half of third ring deactivated

There is a reason I chose this particular scenario for the third and outermost ring. As I puzzled over the circles under consideration, it clicked when that idea landed. I felt as if the crop circle creators were guiding me, through intuition, to do it this way. I had this feeling many times during the entire process of deciphering the formations. Without this feeling I do not believe I could have reached many of the conclusions I did. Besides helping me to come to a greater understanding of the crop circles, I was being taught to trust my inner guidance. For most of my life I had been out of touch with this important aspect of myself. Getting back in touch has given me a strong sense of purpose. Now let's return to the final subject under consideration in this chapter.

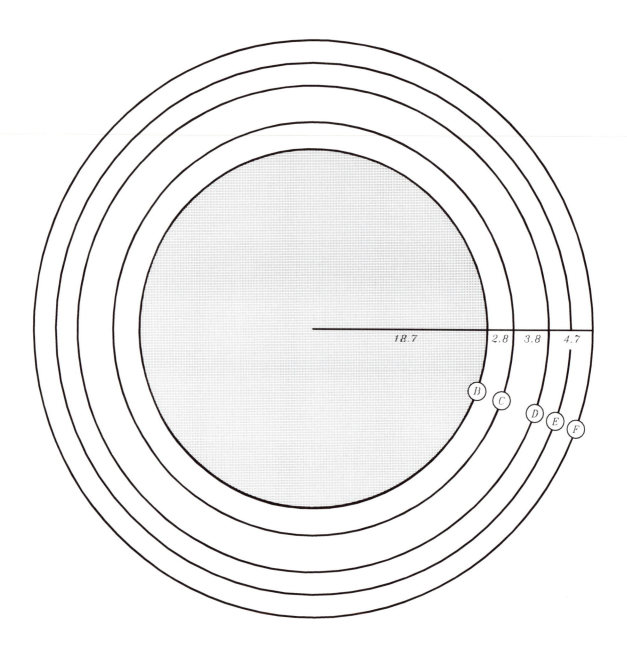

Diagram No. 29: Copy of Diagram 10 of *Bishop Cannings One*

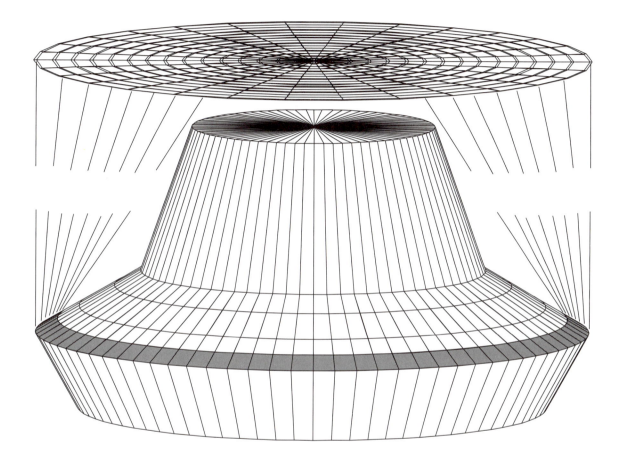

Diagram No. 30A: Copy of Diagram 28D

ROTATING TO THE VERTICAL

Notice in Diagram 30A that the field is established between the outermost ring and the horizontal beam. Diagram 30B indicates that the rotating beam gun has rotated to approximately a forty-five degree angle and the field is following it. Diagram 30C indicates that the beam gun has arrived at its vertical position and the field is intact.

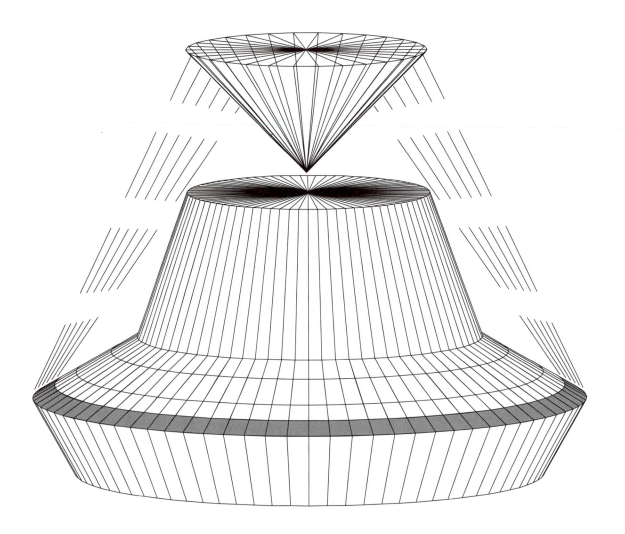

Diagram No. 30B: Beam at forty-five degree angle plus the field

By establishing the field in this manner, not only has less energy been expended, but the resultant field is much weaker. Therefore, the ship will not automatically ascend when the field comes into place. Controlled ascent can be achieved by simply adding power.

This concludes our discussion of ascent. We will now take a look at descent. If I'm going up, I want to know how to get back down — gracefully.

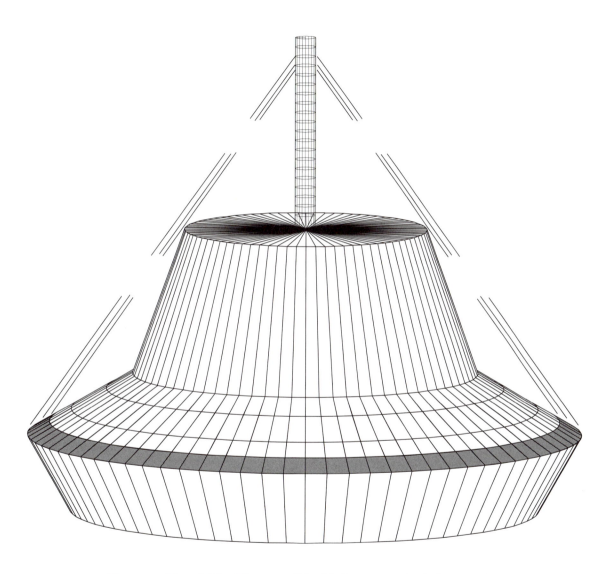

Diagram No. 30C: Diagram 22 with beam vertical plus the field

CHAPTER EIGHT

Descent

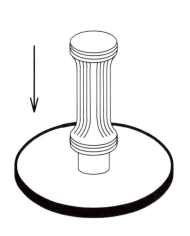

To understand how the ship descends, we need to inspect its lower half. This can be observed in Photo 50. Notice that the lower, outer ring cannot see what is occurring above it on the upper ring due to the ninety degree angled edge. Thus the two rings are *blind* to each other while still sharing a common border. Because the two rings do have a common border, it follows that they would also have a common charge. We have previously determined that the top ring contains a negative charge, therefore, the bottom ring must also have a negative charge. The spinning model of *Newton-St. Lowe* verifies this assumption when a subtle observation is made (See Photo 51). Notice that the key forms the outer ring of both the top and bottom discs. The key is showing us that both discs have the same (negative) charge. When we discuss lateral motion, this common charge to both rings will again be verified.

Take another look at Photo 51, particularly the formidable discharge emanating from the center of the lower disc. This column of energy differs markedly from the slender vertical beam located above the ship. Although both beams differ in appearance, each is composed of spheres. Since the spheres found on and around the vertical beam above the ship were determined to contain a positive charge, it can be assumed that the spheres located below the ship also contain a positive charge. This choice is reinforced by our previous determination that the lower, outer ring contains a negative charge. Opposites attract.

Photo 52 is of *The Gallops* model spinning. Notice that the double-arcs beneath the ship strongly indicate a relationship between the vertical column and the outer ring. This observation is validated by the first insectogram deciphered, *Barn Head,* which clearly indicates that an electromagnetic field exists both above and below the model (See Photo 53). To understand how this field is formed, let's add a couple of features from the *Newton-St. Lowe* and *Barn Head* models to the ship model.

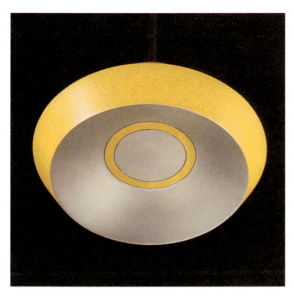

Photo No. 50: Vertical view of model
(lower ring painted)

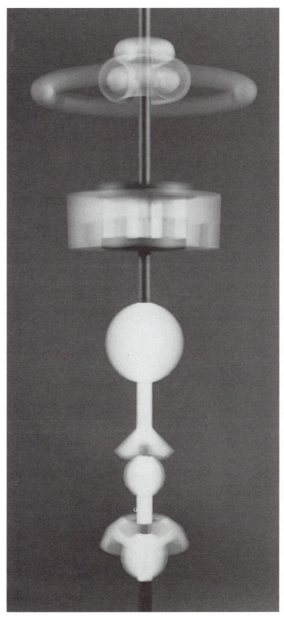

Photo No. 51: *Newton-St.Lowe*
Model Spinning

119

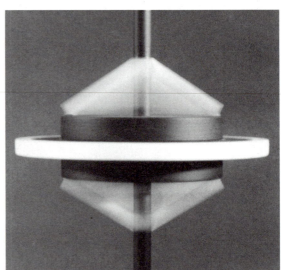

Photo No. 53: Photo 12,
Barn Head model spinning

Photo No. 52: Photo 34,
The Gallops model spinning

In Diagram 31 the lower vertical column from the *Newton-St.Lowe* model has been added to the ship. The two folded antennae from the *Barn Head* model have also been added and are represented by the dashed lines that extend from the outer ring to the bottom sphere. This seemed to be a logical conclusion to me since we have already concluded that the electromagnetic field extends from the center shaft to the outer disc. It is now apparent that the vertical column extending from beneath the ship comprises one terminus of the electromagnetic field.

In Diagram 32 the lower beam from *Fat Boy* has been substituted for the *Newton-St.Lowe* beam. This was done because the *Fat Boy* model depicted the actual shape of the top and bottom beams.

A number of observations can be made about this diagram:

1) The electromagnetic field below the ship has its terminuses located at the outer ring and the center beam. Consequently, the ship will descend for the identical two reasons that it ascended.

   A) The negatively charged, outer ring is attracted to the positively charged beam.

   B) <u>Due to the shape of the ship</u>, the outer ring can see only that portion of the center beam that is located well beneath the ship.

This is all fine and dandy; but why the two totally different approaches to what appears to be an identical process? In other words, why not simply duplicate the top of the ship on the bottom? The answer lies in common sense.

It would appear reasonable that the primary direction the ship travels is forward — or up, as we would think of it. Since it is a space ship, it must travel forward at incredible speeds, thus creating a tremendous amount of kinetic energy. A good analogy would be a freight train traveling at five thousand miles per hour. Common sense dictates that at some point we are going to have to stop this thing and we might want to stop it right now! To accomplish this would require a powerful braking action with instant response. This is exactly what the bottom of the ship is all about. Here is how it works.

The top and bottom outer rings are energized continuously whenever the ship is powered. When the lower beam gun is energized, the electromagnetic field is instantaneously created, resulting in immediate braking. Now, the reasoning behind the very large and powerful vertical beam becomes apparent. Furthermore, the braking rate can be controlled by modulating the intensity of both the beam and the outer ring.

We were supposed to be discussing descent, not braking. In actuality the components are interchangeable. How this is accomplished requires an added dash of common sense.

Obviously, the ship cannot descend solely with the braking components alone, as descent would be extremely rapid. Controlled descent can be achieved, however, by the simultaneous use of both the top and bottom, particle beam guns. Thus, one beam gun can be set at a fixed power setting, while the other is modulated to

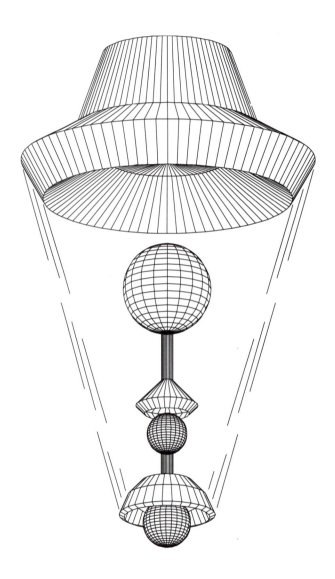

Diagram No. 31: Horizontal view of bottom of ship with lines drawn from outer ring to intersect the lower half of *Newton-St.Lowe.*

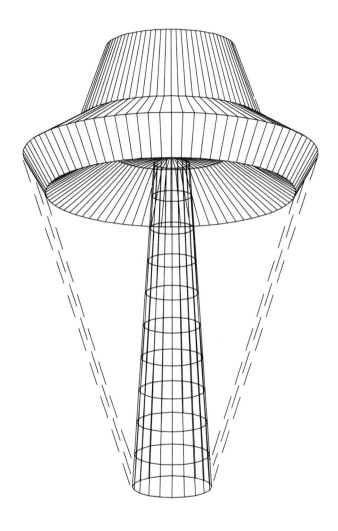

Diagram No. 32: Same as Diagram No. 31 with column in place of *Newton-St.Lowe* and two lines depicting field between outer ring and column.

acquire the desired rate of descent. Photos 54 and 55 depict the ship as it would appear during controlled descent. Both the top and bottom particle beam guns are operating, and both the upper and lower outer rings are energized. Both electromagnetic fields are in place and working in synchronization to acquire controlled descent. This concludes our discussion of descent. We will now address angular motion.

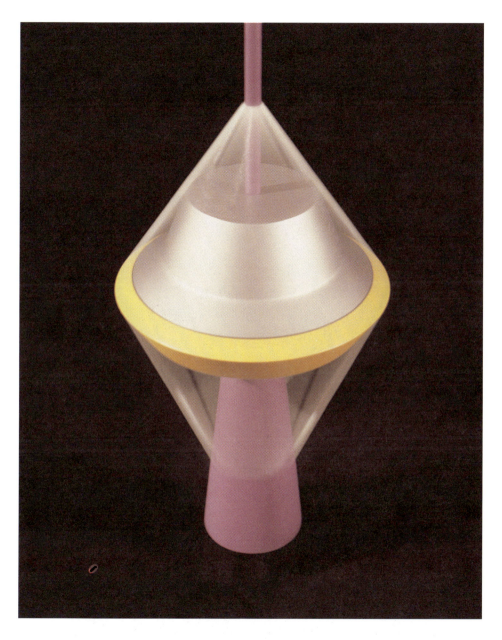

Photo No. 54: Model spinning with top and bottom fields and top and bottom beams to scale. (Top View)

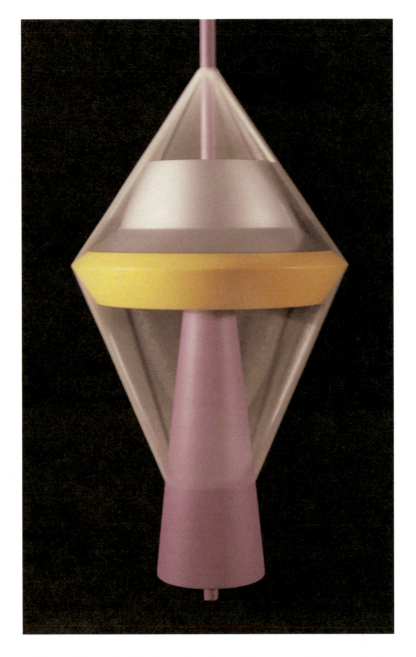

Photo No. 55: Model spinning with top and bottom fields and top and bottom beams to scale. (Side View)

CHAPTER NINE

Angular Motion

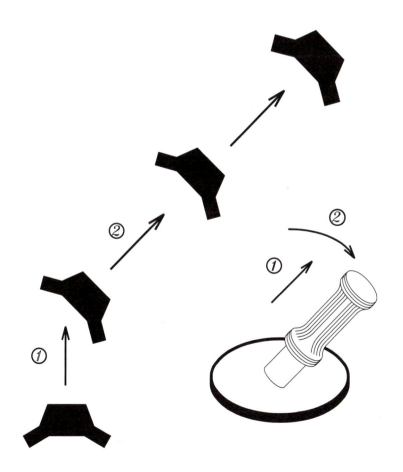

The ship's ability to rotate on its axis enables it to travel at any angle from the vertical. Without this ability, its flight path would be one of right angles. A ridiculous way to travel!

To understand how the ship accomplishes angular motion requires us to revisit two pictograms and decipher two new ones.

A RETURN TO BISHOP CANNINGS TWO
Bottom View

Diagram 33 is of the *Bishop Cannings Two* crop circle. It is identical to Diagram 17 (page 84) except that four circles have been added. These four circles were present in the crop circle. I intentionally did not include them in Diagram 17, as they were not needed then. It might appear to you that I am fiddling with the crop circles and causing confusion. In reality, just the opposite is occurring as I attempt to cut through the maze created by them.

Returning to Diagram 33, notice how these circles are situated directly across from each other and are centered between two rings. The circles are actually discs. These discs are attached to both rings as indicated in the diagram. The two rings rotate along with the four discs. These observations are validated by a specific crop circle.

BISHOP CANNINGS TWO

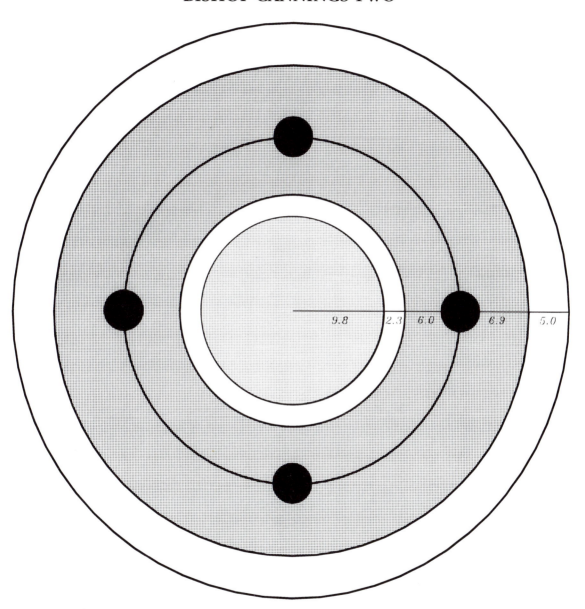

9.8   2.3   6.0   6.9   5.0

Diagram No. 33: Diagram 17 (page 84) with four circles added. The two rings (shaded), rotate along with the four disks.

HACKEN HILL

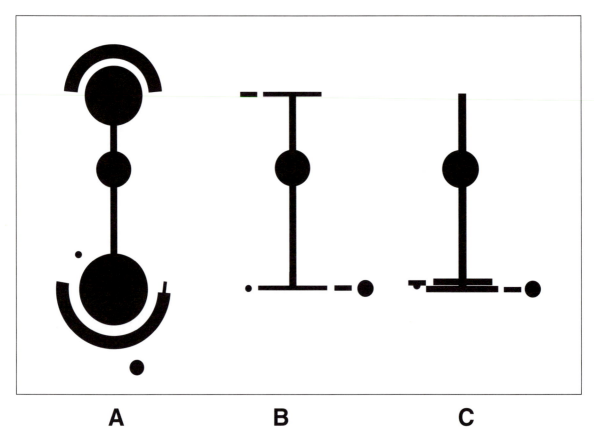

A   B   C

Diagram No. 34: *Hacken Hill*

A) Diagram of the *Hacken Hill* crop circle as it appeared in the field.

B) The discs have been rotated ninety degrees. The arcs around both discs, along with the two floating spheres, rotate with the discs and remain in their respective positions. Only the left side of the top arc is shown for clarity. Only the right side of the bottom arc is shown for clarity.

C) The top disc has been moved down the shaft, past the sphere located on the shaft, until it rests against the lower disc. There is no spacer. The model is a pancake. Notice how the small sphere on the left must be cut in half to accomodate the top disc and its associated arc.

HACKEN HILL
created July 12, 1991

The *Hacken Hill* pictogram is a complex derivative of the dumbbell pictograms. It took me a long time to decipher this formation and a longer time to understand its message.

Diagram 34 depicts the process of deciphering the *Hacken Hill* pictogram. Figure (A) is a drawing of the formation, while figure (B) indicates that the two discs, along with their floating spheres, have been rotated ninety degrees. Figure (C) indicates that the smaller, top disc has been slid down the shaft, past the sphere in the middle of the shaft, until it contacts the larger disc. There is not a spacer in the formation! This realization was difficult for me to accept until I understood what the formation was communicating. Before we discuss that, let's complete assembly of the model.

Without a spacer, the discs lay one on top of the other. This immediately caused another problem. The small floating sphere, located directly beneath the smaller disc, will no longer fit — as a sphere. I fiddled with the model for quite a while before realizing that the small sphere must be cut in half in order for the two discs to fit flush (See Photo 58). This seemed very strange at the time, but I believe it was exactly what the crop circle creators intended.

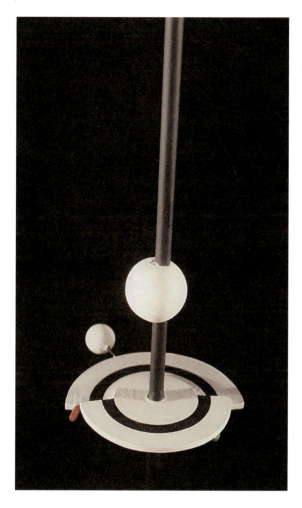

Photo No. 56: Model Stationary
(Top View)

HACKEN HILL

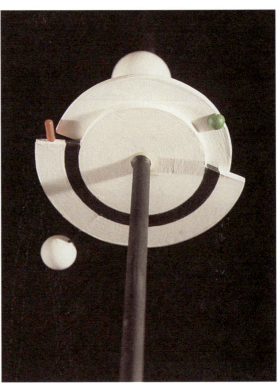

Photo No. 58: Model Stationary
(Bottom View)

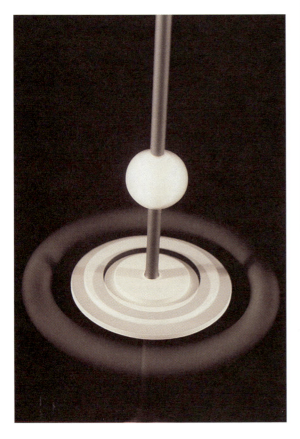

Photo No. 57: Model Spinning
(Top View)

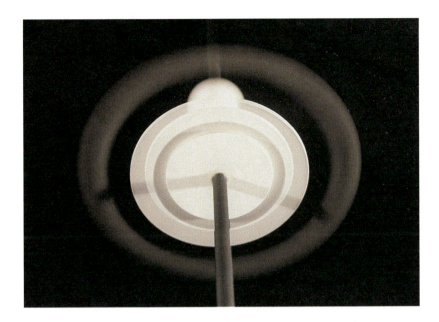

Photo No. 59:
Model Spinning
(Bottom View)

Photo 59 is of the bottom of the model spinning. Unfortunately, the camera wasn't capable of capturing what I intended to observe at this point. As I mentioned earlier, the crop circle creators designed their formations to be deciphered and spun by a computer. If I had access to such technology, you would surely have it, however, in its absence I will explain what should be observed. Please refer to Photos 58 and 59 as I run through this.

The appendage on the outer disc creates the illusion of the angled, outer ring while the half-sphere is conveying two pieces of information.

1) As the model spins, its location is observed to be in the middle of the two rings.

2) It is seen as a blur and represents the four discs rotating on the two rings. This small half-sphere is telling us that the four discs aren't discs at all, but half-spheres, or domes. The spinning model is telling us that the two rings and the four domes rotate with the discs.

These domes house electrical components that are used to create angular motion. The use of domes makes sense because electrical components located on the exterior of the ship would require protection from the elements.

Now let's finish up this model by quickly discussing its top portion. Photo 57 is of the top of the model spinning. Again, we are presented with the relationship between the sphere on the vertical shaft and the spinning floating-sphere at the edge of the model. We already know about this relationship between the vertical beam and the outer ring; however, the crop circle creators don't miss an opportunity to reinforce their teachings. Now let's return to an old friend, Stonehenge, to add its knowledge to the bottom of the ship.

STONEHENGE REVISITED

The spinning model of *Stonehenge* revealed that the ladder transformed into a perfect energy field that originated at the center of the ship and extended outward to its edge (See Photos 60 and 61). Now that we know the actual shape of the bottom of the ship, and that the center area contains a vertical-beam gun, we can add the knowledge which *Stonehenge* provides to it.

1) The ladder must represent a beam.
2) In order for this beam to exist, there must be a second beam gun located at the center of the ship.
3) The gun must rotate, just as the ladder had to rotate to form its field.
4) Since both previous beam guns fired a positively-charged beam, this beam is probably also positively charged. This supposition appears to be correct, as the beam passes very close to the lower, negatively charged, outer ring. This will be validated when we discuss stabilization.

We now have a vertical beam gun and a rotating beam gun located at the center of the ship's bottom. It would not seem prudent to

have these electronic guns exposed to the elements. A special crop circle supplies us with just the right cover for them.

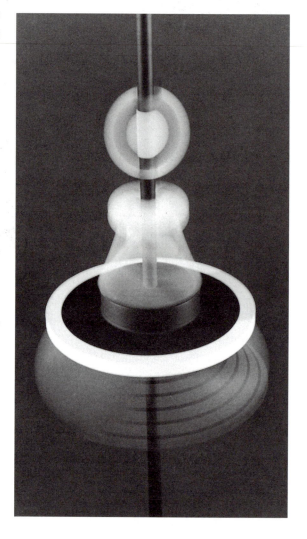

Photo No. 60: Copy of Photo 16
(*Stonehenge*)

Photo No. 61: Copy of Photo 17 (*Stonehenge*)

THE WOODFORD SIX-RINGER

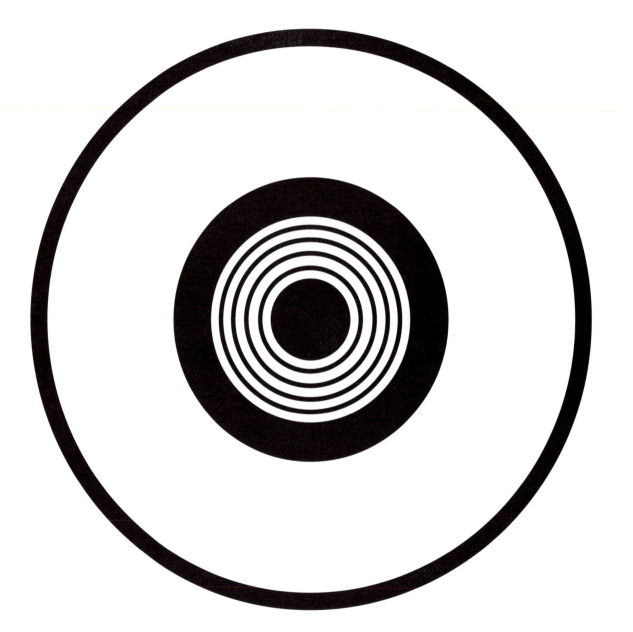

Diagram No. 35: The *Woodford* Six-Ringer

THE WOODFORD SIX-RINGER
date of creation - unknown

This crop circle is a dead giveaway. It depicts the bottom of the ship and concentrates on the center area. I diagramed this photograph to a scale of six inches (See Diagram 35). Notice the series of tightly compressed rings near the center of the diagram. These rings indicate a circular, vertical structure that is located in the middle of the bottom disc. Such a structure would be represented by a dome. The inner-most area of these circles represents the circumference of the vertical beam as it departs the dome. Common sense tells me that the dome is a full dome, as the beam guns are electronic and would fire through it.

Photo 62 (next page) depicts the bottom of the ship. The center dome and ladder, along with the four opposing domes, and the inner and outer rings are in place. The inner ring will be discussed shortly, which is the reason it is included at this time.

The model now contains all the components required for angular motion. First, however, we should be aware that any time the ships' systems are powered, the following components are always operating:

1) The upper and lower, outer rings;
2) The top beam;
3) The electromagnetic field above the ship;
4) The lower, rotating beam gun rotates and forms its positively charged field;
5) The four opposing domes rotate with their associated two rings.

Now, to understand angular motion let's go out the back door and sit at the controls of our ship. In short order, we are slowly ascending vertically. To rotate the ship to a 45-degree angle, we would bend the control handle to the right at a 45-degree angle. Beneath the ship, the four domes are rotating on their double rings and doing absolutely nothing. The ship's systems would respond in the following manner. As we signal for a 45-degree angular change, a certain fixed point beneath the ring is electronically marked. This fixed point would coincide exactly with the direction in which the control handle was bent. Every time one of the rotating domes passes over this stationary point it would become energized with a negative charge. While the dome is negatively charged, it is attracted to the positive field hovering just above it. This positive field is created by the rotating beam gun at the center of the ship. This all happens very rapidly and the ship would be perceived to rotate smoothly as dome after dome passes over the fixed point and is energized, thus turning the ship slightly.

The ship's rotation rate can be controlled by modulating the rotation speed of the domes, as well as modulating the power to the rotating beam and domes. Naturally, the ship is capable of angular motion in any direction. In other words, the control handle can be moved to any point within a 360-degree radius and the ship will rotate in that direction. This is because the

THE GIFT

direction in which the control handle is bent is duplicated by the fixed point over which the ring of domes passes. The angle to which the ship will rotate is controlled by the angle of the control handle. Once the ship has reached this angle, the fixed point beneath the ring will be de-energized. However, the two discs and the domes will continue to rotate. Instant re-

sponse to any angular change signal is assured as long as the rotating beam gun is operating, which it does continuously whenever the ship is powered.

A secondary reason for the beam gun's continuous operation is to stabilize the ship. To understand this aspect we will revisit two familiar crop circles.

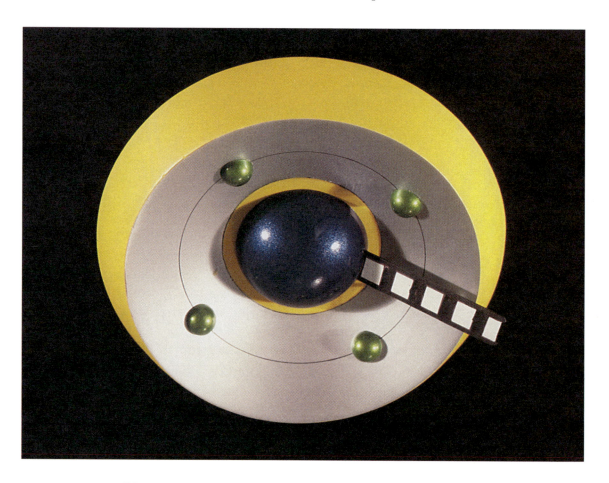

Photo No. 62: Vertical bottom view of model stationary with dome, ladder, and four domes added.

CHAPTER TEN

Stabilization and Lateral Motion

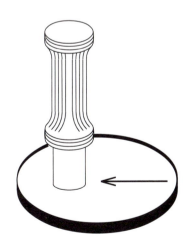

STABILIZATION

Consider for a moment the number of components on the ship that are rotating:

1) The top beam gun rotates at certain times.
2) The lower rotating-beam gun rotates continuously.
3) The four domes and their associated discs rotate continuously.
4) There is yet another rotating component of the ship that will be discussed shortly.

If we add all of these rotating components up, it becomes obvious that the ship has an inherent stability problem. I can tell you with confidence that the ship does not contain any stabilizing gyros. Rather, it is stabilized by an energy field (page 138).

Please return to Photo 62 (Page 138) and note the inner, orange ring that circumscribes the center dome. The only reason for this ring's existence is to stabilize the ship. It is continuously energized with a negative charge whenever the ship is powered for flight. Thus, it is constantly attracted to the positive field hovering above it that is being formed by the rotating beam gun. Notice that this ring is very close to the center of the ship where the rotating beam is strongest. This central location provides an ideal position for the ring to maintain a firm, stabilizing grip on the ship.

There is a second stabilizing ring present beneath the ship. It is the outer ring that absorbs the remaining energy of the rotating-beam. Thus, the outer ring serves as a secondary stabilizer while the inner ring is the primary stabilizer.

This concludes our discussion of stabilization. The only function remaining is lateral motion and I have a pleasant surprise for you.

LATERAL MOTION
LEWIS SUSSEX

Diagram No. 36: *Lewis, Sussex* from *Dowsing The Crop Circles.*
Drawing by Roland Pargeter.

LATERAL MOTION

The *Lewis, Sussex* crop circle does not require deciphering. What you see is what you get. I discovered it in **Dowsing The Crop Circles**. The formation provides us with a snapshot of lateral motion.

Diagram 36 is of the *Lewis, Sussex* crop circle. It provides us with a vertical view of the top of the ship. The two sets of lines connecting the ship with the small circle represent two beams being fired from their respective beam gun. Each of these beam guns is located at the edge of the ship and fires at a fixed angle. The guns are firing a positively charged particle beam that, by itself, does not interact with the negatively charged upper and lower outer rings of the ship. However, when the beams collide a tremendous amount of energy is released, creating the large spheres located just beyond their intersection point. The upper and lower outer rings are immediately attracted to this wall of positively charged particles causing the ship to move laterally.

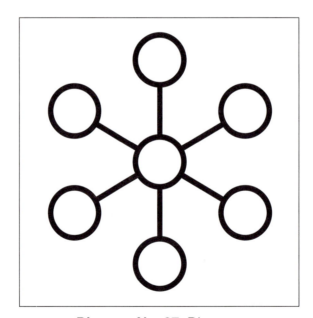

Diagram No. 37: Diagram
of a crop circle created
during the summer of 1993.

Diagrams 37 and 38A are of a crop circle that appeared during the summer of 1993. It indicates six outer circles that are all interconnected as through the spokes of a wheel. When this diagram is overlaid onto Diagram 36, the result is 38C. Notice that two of the circles overlay the origination points of the two beams perfectly. Given a little more thought, a picture emerges of what is occurring here.

The six circles represent beam gun pods that contain not one but two beam guns. Now, let's add these guns to the pods depicted in 38C. The result is 38D. This brings the entire exercise into focus.

Let's take a short field trip to the ship to understand lateral motion. We are now in the ship and ascending vertically at a slow rate. To move the ship horizontally to the right, we would move the control column horizontally to the right. The ship's systems would respond in the following manner :

1) Our control column signal would electronically mark a point beneath the hub from which the spokes extend.

2) Each time a point midway between two of the spokes crosses this marked point the two inward-facing beam guns would fire.

3) This continuous firing cycle of each set of inward-facing beam guns would create a positively charged field a specific distance from the ship.

4) The negatively charged, upper and lower, outer rings would be attracted to the positively charged field and the ship would move horizontally towards it.

5) This horizontal motion would be in the identical direction as commanded by the control column.

6) The ship would continue to travel horizontally until the control lever was either returned to its neutral position or another lateral direction selected.

The ship's systems offer instantaneous response to a horizontal input from the control column. This is achieved by the spoked wheel rotating continuously any time the ship is powered for flight. We have already established that the upper and lower, outer rings are continuously energized anytime the ship is powered for flight. Therefore, the only remaining requirement for acquiring horizontal motion would be the firing of the beam guns. That happens instantaneously as indicated.

This concludes our discussion of the various functions of the ship and its related systems. I have provided an additional photo of the ship as it would appear if you walked up to it (See Photo 63). This is a photo of the ship's underside with the central dome and four smaller domes in place. Photos 42 and 43 on pages 89 and 90 provide other views. Likewise, only one additional photo of the bottom of the ship, as it would appear in full operation, is required. (See Photo No. 64 on page 146.) The other views are provided in Photos 54 and 55 on pages 125 and 126. Naturally these fields would be invisible to us, however, the spinning models reveal them to us.

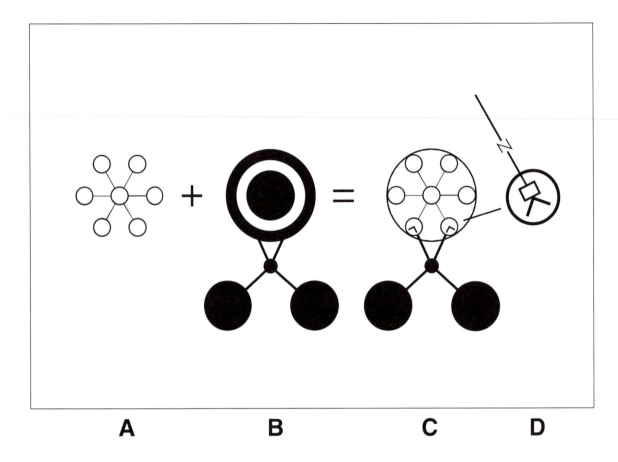

Diagram No. 38: Combination of two crop circles

A) A copy of Diagram 37.

B) A copy of the *Lewis Sussex* crop circle presented in Diagram 36.

C) The sum of adding Diagrams A and B. Notice that two of the pods line up perfectly with the beams extending out from the large disc.

D) A blowup of a pod indicating the two beam guns contained within each pod.

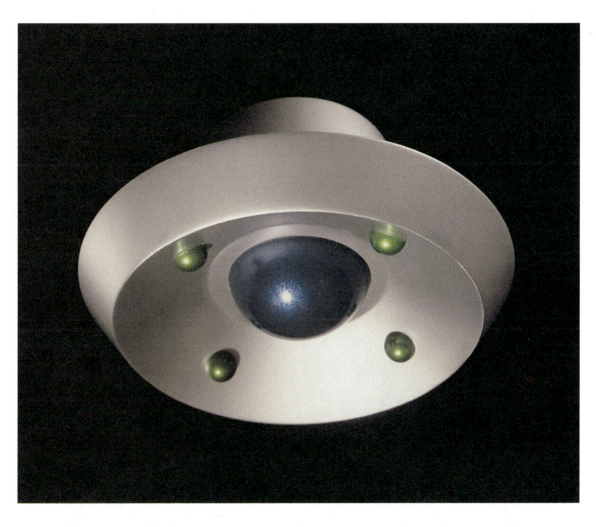

Photo No. 63: Ship's underside as it would appear if you walked up to it.

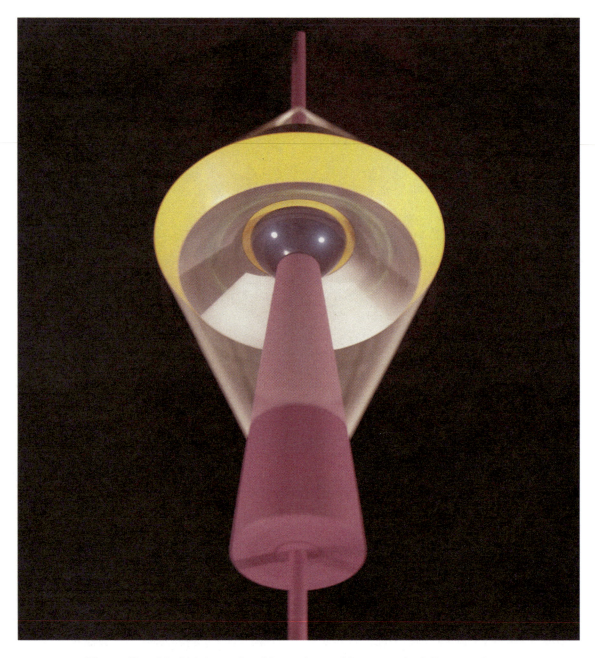

Photo No. 64: Ship's underside as it would appear in full operation.
The fields would actually be invisible.

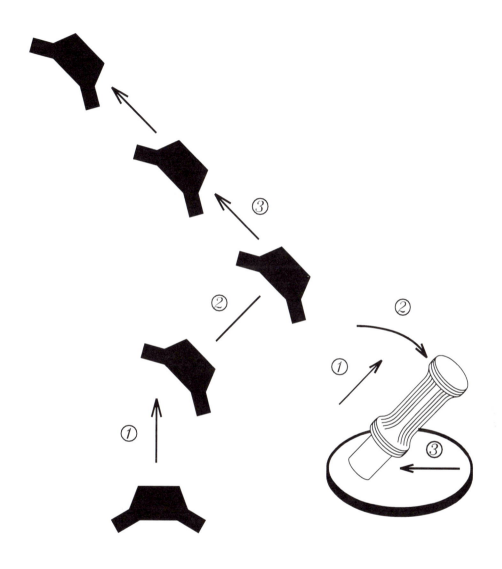

Combining Maneuvers:
1) Vertical ascent
2) Angular motion
3) Horizontal motion or "slip"

CHAPTER ELEVEN

Power Plant

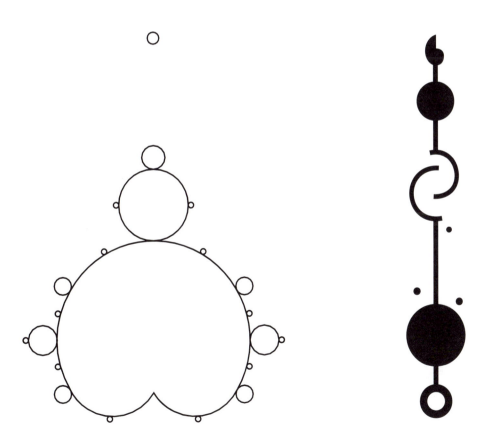

All the crop circles we have looked at so far were created in 1990 and 1991. As we have seen, these formations related to the ship and its various functions. We learned that spheres, or particles, are fired from specific points on the ship and are attracted to particular areas around the exterior of the ship. However, none of these crop circles addressed the power plant or the particles involved. This all changed during the summers of 1992, 1993 and 1994 when the majority of the formations focused on just these subjects.

Unfortunately, these crop circles never received the tremendous circulation that the 1990 and 1991 crop formations did. This was due to the announcement by two Englishmen in 1991 that they had created the crop circles. News of the apparent hoax was broadcast worldwide and interest rapidly dissipated.

I possess a number of these formations and we will take a look at them. To fully understand the ship's power plant and the particle, or particles, involved will require all the 1992, 1993, 1994 and 1995 crop circles. As you will soon see, the crop circles formed during these later years assume a different appearance from their predecessors. The simpler formations communicate a novel, particle-physics language that, once understood, can be applied to the more complex formations. Our scientists will then be able to read the more complex formations as easily as you are reading this book. In the meantime, I can provide an adequate insight to these crop circles related to the functions of the ship.

THE PATH OF LIGHT

As the time approached to write this chapter it became apparent that I needed to talk with someone acquainted with nuclear physics or electromagnetism. Through a friend, I located an electrical engineer who specializes in electromagnetism. The two of us met for lunch and spent the afternoon kicking this thing around. During our talk, we arrived at the conclusion that the ship must be powered by a neutral particle, or particles. Our decision was based on the following abbreviated discussion.

1) If the ship's fields were electromagnetic, they would have to be very powerful to propel a ship of such mass.

2) Therefore, the fields would carry an extremely strong charge.

3) If the ship flew low over one of our towns or cities, it would bend any metal post such as a street sign. It might even rip them out of the ground and become covered by them, similar to a magnet in a box of paper clips. Furthermore, these ships have been observed by scuba divers in the ocean. Visibility in the ocean is, at best, two hundred feet, which places the scuba diver within two hundred feet of the ship. The scuba diver would experience an electrical shock of such magnitude that death could occur, and large fish kills would be the order of the day.

4) I know that these beings would not harm a

fly. Therefore, the primary particle associated with the power source does not contain a charge. It is a neutral particle and the energy field it creates is also neutral.

5) To my knowledge, such a field does not exist on this planet today.

As our conversation continued, it was evident that my acquaintance understood all of my drawings and explanations perfectly. However, I could sense that he was baffled by this extraordinary power source as well as the particle's identity. Then our discussion suddenly took a ninety degree turn as he began speaking about light, its properties, and how it acted. He concluded with the statement that the field of particle physics was, at this moment, upside down. The scientists were having a tough time making heads or tails of their observations.

This was not good news for me and I guess he could read my thoughts through my expression. Understanding my predicament, he offered a suggestion. There was a theoretical physicist by the name of Richard Feynman who very likely could help me. He related that Feynman prided himself in communicating as simply and straightforward as humanly possible with his fellow man. This appealed to me because I knew how close I was to becoming a Daffy Duck. Even more appealing was his next statement that Feynman had written a book for the nonscientific community called *QED*. After our meeting I went to the library and took out a copy of *QED*.

QED is cute. Quantum Electrodynamics is not. The theory of quantum electrodynamics that Richard Feynman and two other scientists perfected accounts for all the phenomena occurring in the physical world, excluding gravity and radioactivity. I have never met professor Feynman, and I will not quote any portion of his book. However, the book captivated me and contained the exact information I required.

1) I learned that light appears to travel in a straight line because this is the path of least time. In reality, light travels in an infinite number of directions. However, light not gathered about the perceived line of least time cancels itself out through interference.

2) Light is composed of particles called photons. Photons are counted among the fundamental particles of which all matter is composed.

3) The manner in which electromagnetism and light act is very similar.

These three observations lit up like a light bulb in my mind.

Early on I had deciphered a crop circle that made no sense to me, however, after learning these facts about light, things came slamming together. Let's take a look at this crop circle.

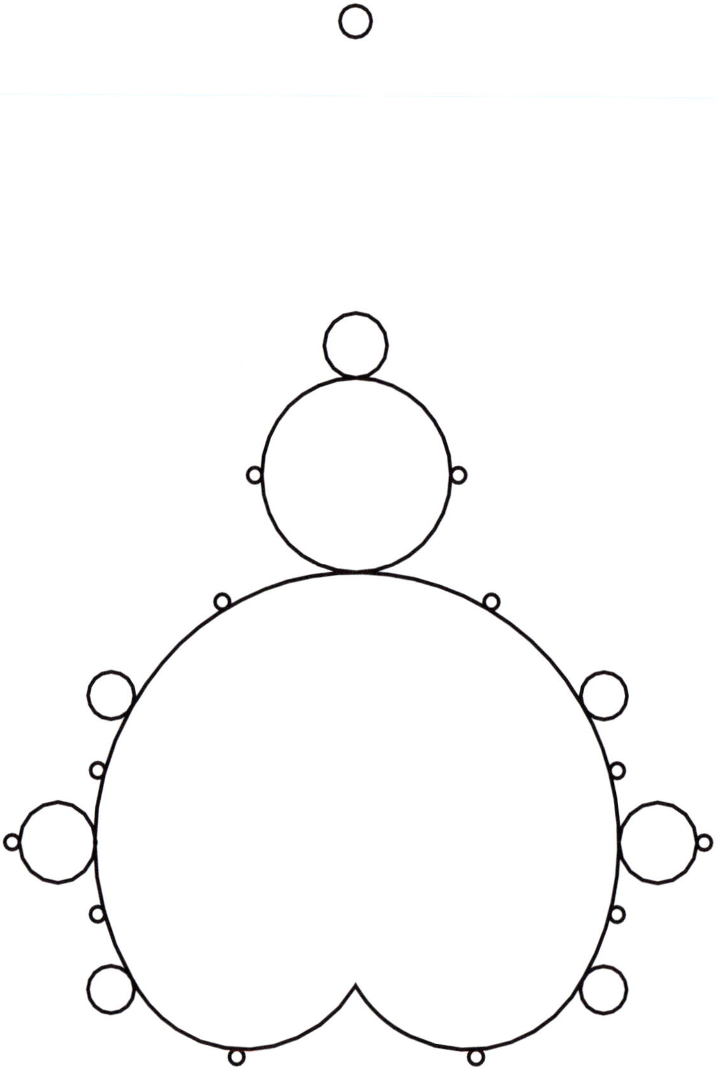

Diagram No. 39: *Mandelbrot* formation

THE MANDELBROT SET,
created August 12, 1991

This formation closely resembles a mathematical model known as the *Mandelbrot Set,* named after its creator, Benoit B. Mandelbrot. The mathematical model is one of a number of diagrams that evolved from the study of fractal geometry — an area of mathematics associated with Chaos Theory. Shortly after the discovery of the formation, the English properly named it after its mathematical counterpart.

The formation does not require decipherment as it is another case of what-you-see-is-what-you-get. A model was constructed by cutting the formation out of a sheet of plywood and mounting the spheres to it. The model was then attached to a shaft and promptly spun (See Diagram 40 and Photo 65). When observed spinning, this simple model transformed into a beautiful, three dimensional form that completely took me by surprise.

It was not until reading *QED* that I realized what the *Mandelbrot Set* was communicating. The crop circle creators were indicating, in dramatic fashion, the outer limits of the actual particle field enveloping the ship.

The only problem was the absence of the ship. To add the ship, I drew a scale model with only one requirement. The perimeter of the center disc must contact the two large spheres located at the outer edges of the *Mandelbrot Set* model. I then gave Al the plans and asked him to make the model and then cut it in half.

Please understand that Al painstakingly creates these saucers out of a solid piece of wood. I thought he would object to chopping this one in half. I was surprised by his quick reply of "Okay," and surmised that he had created so many extraordinary pieces in the past few months that my request did not even faze him.

After he completed his part, I painted the two halves and attached one to each side of the *Mandelbrot.*

Photo 66 is of the spinning *Mandelbrot Set* model with the addition of the ship. Notice how the spheres are drawn towards the outer rings of the upper and lower, center disc. Most importantly, the spheres are moving in a modified circular fashion towards the center disc. We are witnessing the outer perimeter of a controlled particle field gratis the *Mandelbrot Set.* To understand this, let's revert to the mathematical model for a moment (See Diagram 39). The mathematical model illustrates visually all the area that is known or controlled. This area encompasses everything within the *Mandelbrot,* while all the area outside the formation is uncontrolled, or random.

In other words, as the particles are fired within their beams from above and below the ship, those particles located within the *Mandelbrot* are being attracted to the outer ring of the ship and are controlled. Our perception of this movement is a straight line along a path of least time, which is portrayed in the spinning

Diagram No. 40: *Mandelbrot* spinning

Photo No. 65: Model Spinning

Photo No. 66: Model with outline of ship spinning

models of the ship (See Photos 54 and 55 on pages 125 and 126). These fields were derived from a number of crop circle models of which the *Barn Head* model depicts them best (See Photos 11 and 12, pages 30 and 31). Conversely, many of the crop circle models depicted the particles moving in a pattern closely resembling the *Mandelbrot Set,* and thus were illustrating their actual paths (See Photos 26 and 27 on page 52 and Photos 29, 30, and 31 on pages 57 and 58).

As you can see, a mere perusal of particle physics produced immediate results and cleared up an apparent paradox. Just imagine what will happen when our scientists become involved! All of a sudden their years of hard work and studying will pay off in an unprecedented manner.

THE PARTICLE

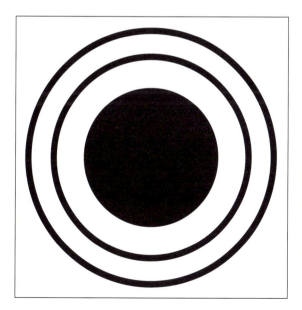

Diagram No. 41   **Diagram No. 42**

THE PARTICLE

While the crop circles of 1990 and 1991 did not specifically address the primary particle responsible for propelling the ship, they did offer us one good look at it. It is the ringed-sphere in Photo 30 on page 58. Take a look at this photo and then take a look at Diagram 41. *Voilá!* They are identical. Now look at Diagram 42 that contains two ringed-particles. One of the particles remains attached to the nucleus of the atom, while the other is separated from it. When I applied my limited knowledge of particle physics to these observations, an apparent match emerged. Here are my thoughts that prompted this apparent match.

The nucleus of an atom is composed of protons, neutrons, neutrinos, quarks, photons, gluons, and W-particles. Of all these particles, the quark caught my attention. The quark is a name allocated to a group of particles numbering in the hundreds. There are two fundamental categories of quarks that are:

A) Baryons are composed of three quarks.

B) Mesons are composed of a quark and an anti-quark.

Quarks have a number of pronounced characteristics that are listed below.

1) All particles composed of quarks are neutral in charge. We are looking for a neutral particle.

2) Quarks are found within the nucleus of atoms. Electromagnetic force holds the electrons in orbit; but particles within the nucleus are controlled by nuclear force. Nuclear force is hundreds or thousands of times greater than electromagnetic force; therefore it requires a much greater force to dislodge a quark from an atom than it does to remove an electron. Once dislodged, the force drawing them back is also much greater. It is this force that powers the ship.

3) The interaction between quarks and gluons produces a very powerful reaction.

4) When the nucleus of an atom is bombarded by a high energy source, a lone quark is never released. Instead, a jet of mesons and baryons is ejected.

When I compared these observations with Photo 30, Diagram 41, and especially Diagram 42, I saw a match.

Diagram 42 contains two ringed-particles. If these two particles compose a quark, then, by definition, that quark is a meson. Now, notice in Diagram 42 that one of the quarks has been separated from the nucleus. Our scientists tell us that this is impossible, yet here we see it. Let's proceed into the power plant to get an idea of how they are stripping a half-meson away from the nucleus of an atom.

OLDBURY CASTLE,
created August 8, 1993

The *Oldbury Castle* pictogram is a stunning formation that addresses the ship's power plant. Please refer to Diagram 44 as we decipher it. Diagram 44A depicts the crop circle as it appeared in the field. Reading the three discs from top to bottom, there is a top disc, a center disc and a bottom disc. This is classic *Alton Barnes* style; nothing tricky here. In Diagram 44B the three discs have been rotated ninety degrees. In Diagram 44C, the three discs have been moved inward. Notice that the top and center discs stop when they contact the two half rings, or calipers. From now on I will be referring to these two half rings as calipers.

Again, in classic *Alton Barnes* style, the bottom disc lies flush with the bottom of the center disc. In Diagram 44D, the top of the model has been rotated toward you, allowing you to view its bottom. Notice in Diagram 44A that the comma, located at the very top of the formation, has moved down the shaft until it meets the top disc. The two floating-spheres positioned next to the vertical shaft remain in their respective positions. The third sphere is located next to the center disc and rotates with the center disc. Now let's take a look at the model spinning. Here is where things get interesting.

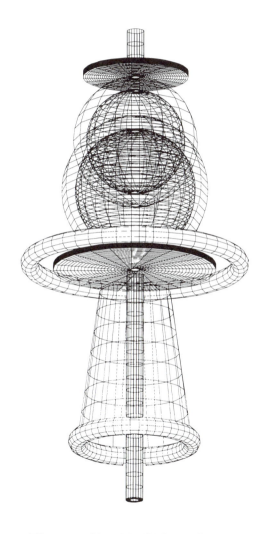

Diagram No. 43: *Oldbury Castle*
(Three dimensional drawing)

159

OLDBURY CASTLE

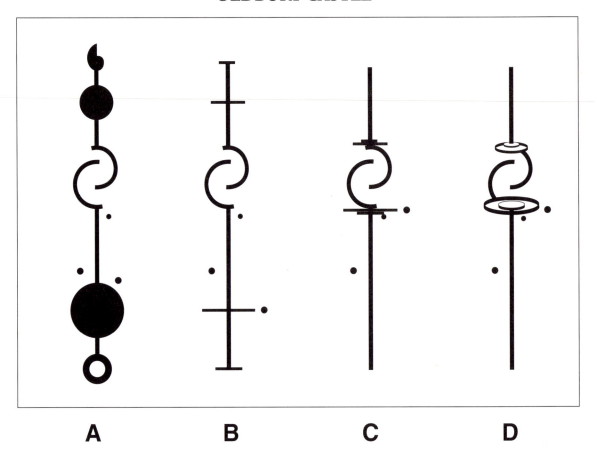

A   B   C   D

Diagram No. 44: *Oldbury Castle*

A) Diagram of *Oldbury Castle* crop circle as it appeared in the field.
B) The three discs have been rotated ninety degrees.
C) The three discs have been moved inward until meeting the two half rings.
D) The model has been rotated toward you, allowing you to view its bottom.

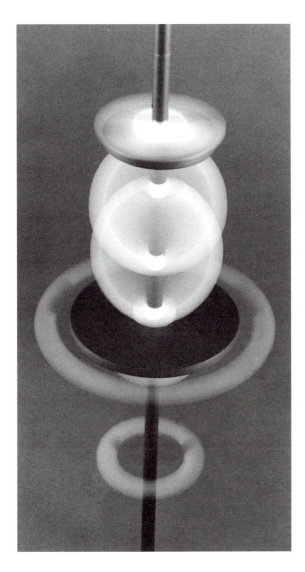

Photo No. 68: Model Spinning
(Top View)

We will begin at the top of the model and work our way down. In Photos 68 and 69 the inner portion of the comma has transformed into a solid, round structure, while the outer area is transparent. We are witnessing the emergence of the particles from the top of the ship.

The mid portion of the model is where everything is happening. Here we are seeing, for the first time, an atomic engine that drives a space ship. I believe that I have this thing figured out — to a point, and then it loses me. Here is what I see.

To begin, the two calipers exist just as you see them in Diagram 44C. As they spin, they form three distinct chambers. The calipers are capable of doing this because they form an electromagnetic field as they spin (See Photos 70, 71). Notice that if the middle chamber is cut horizontally in half, each half is almost a mirror image of each other. I say almost, because the bottom chamber is larger than the top chamber. This makes sense, as the top beam is much smaller than the bottom beam that requires the most power.

For discussion's sake, only the bottom half of the central chamber will be addressed, as each half is essentially a mirror image of the other. As I see it, a jet of atomic particles is injected into the spinning, central chamber and accelerated rapidly to a terminal velocity. This terminal velocity is predicated by the speed, or energy, required for the particles to pass through the central chamber's electromagnetic wall and enter the outer chamber. If you will take a

OLDBURY CASTLE

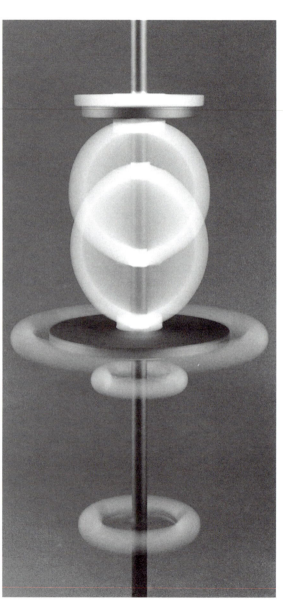

Photo No. 69: Model Spinning
(Top View)

Photo No. 70: Model Spinning
(Side View)

OLDBURY CASTLE

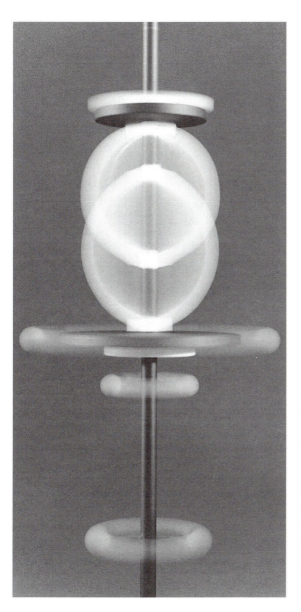

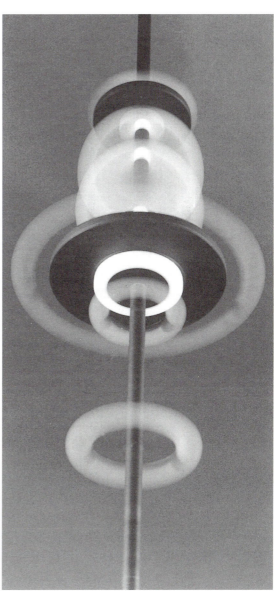

Photo No. 71: *Oldbury Castle*
Side Spinning

Photo No. 72: *Oldbury Castle*
Bottom Spinning

moment to study Photos 70 and 71, you will see that the outer chamber is spinning in the opposite direction of the central chamber, thus instantaneously doubling the speed of the particles. At the instant the particles pass through the central chamber's wall they undergo two distinct operations simultaneously and instantaneously.

1) What happens is that they pass through a specifically-formed, electromagnetic field and double their speed. When the particles pass through the central chamber's electromagnetic field their innate bonding power is overcome.

2) This happens as the shearing effect created by their immediate, rapid acceleration breaks up the nuclei, creating a profusion of particles. Most importantly, single quarks from a meson are present.

The trick now is to produce a steady stream of half-meson particles to be emitted from the bottom of the chamber. Notice in Photos 70 and 71 that the outer chambers taper to a point that resemble a nozzle or venturi. The half-meson particles are being forced to the bottom of the outer chamber by simultaneously being acted upon by the centrifugal force created by the spinning chamber as well as its shape. In order for this nozzle to permit only half-mesons to escape, it must be very special. Fortunately, there is a crop circle that offers us a good idea about how this is accomplished.

Diagram 45 indicates a sphere in the middle of a triangle. The sphere would represent a half-meson particle while the lines of the tri-

Diagram No. 45

angle represent three, crisscrossing, electromagnetic fields. These crisscrossing fields form a filter that allows only a particle of specific dimensions to pass through it. This type of function is known as polarization and it produces polarized particles. In this instance the polarized particle would be a half-meson. Thus, the ship's beams are comprised of half-meson particles. Once the half-mesons have ascended within their beam to a point above the ship where they can see their counterpart located on the outer ring of the ship, they leave the beam and travel towards the outer ring. Thus, this stream of in-transit, half-meson particles creates the neutral energy field enveloping the ship.

In the previous paragraph I stated that the

half-mesons travel from the vertical beam towards their counterparts located on the outer ring of the ship. Herein lies a paradox. Please refer to Diagram 46, which is a copy of Diagram 42 that depicts a split meson. While the single, half-meson particle is fired out of the ship within the vertical beam, the nucleus, along with the other half of the meson, remains within the outer chamber. I do not understand how the nucleus, with its half-meson particle, is transported to the outer ring of the ship where it is required for its polarity. There must be, but I have not yet seen, the crop circle (or circles), that show how this happens. This point really baffles me and constitutes the limit of my understanding of the power plant. However, there is one very interesting observation I would like to make.

A specific quark known as a meson is used to power the ship. This particle is split, creating polarized particles that later become reunited. That is, the half-meson particle travels from the beam, to the outer ring, to the engine, and back out the beam again. Notice that the entire

Diagram No. 46: Split Meson
Copy of Diagram 42

ship is involved within this closed circuit. The ship has just revealed itself to be an energy machine that would not require fuel for a very long time, if ever! With this said, I would like to introduce a few additional, interesting discoveries that are offered without explanation.

THE OVERTON FORMATION
created in August, 1993

This formation resembles the very familiar handicapped parking signs. There is a little trick to deciphering the formation. The half-ring does not rotate ninety degrees around its center in the usual fashion. Rather, it rotates from its lowest point (See Diagram 47B), while the top disc rotates ninety degrees around the

center shaft in the usual manner. In Diagram 47C the top disc has moved inward until reaching the center sphere. That is all there is to it. I did not make a model of this deciphered formation as I had to stop somewhere. Instead, Fred created a, three-dimensional, computer-animated drawing of the model that could be built from this formation. Astounding results as you can see in Diagram 48.

This diagram bowled me over. As I looked at this drawing, several thoughts raced through my mind simultaneously:

1) What other crop circles that I had deciphered did this process apply to?

2) Am I witnessing yet another dimension within the crop circles?

3) What was this thing?

My first thought provoked an initial reaction that I had totally missed an entire side to the crop circles. Slowly, it became apparent that I had not. All the previous crop circles, except

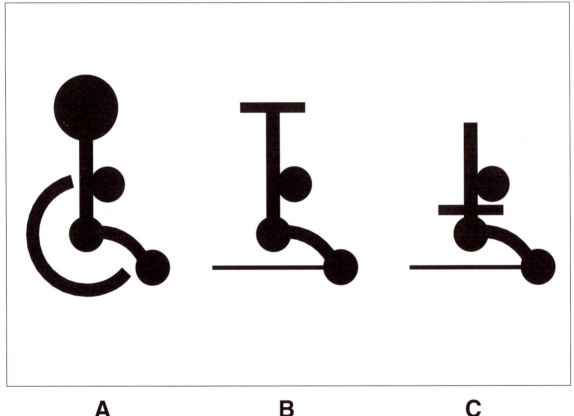

A   **B**   **C**

Diagram No. 47: The *Overton* formation

A) The *Overton* formation as it appeared in the field.

B) The half-ring rotates from its lowest point and the top disc rotates ninety degrees around the center shaft.

C) The top disc has moved inward until meeting the center sphere.

one, were meant to be spun as I had done. The one exception was the *Barbury Castle* formation found on pages 104-107. This formation had bugged me from the onset. I always knew there was more there than I was seeing. In particular, the three complex outer circles were not created merely to be spun in their horizontal position. I now understood that these outer circles were meant to be spun independently of the rotating cone. By doing this, they would form spheres and offer excellent insight to the particle, or particles, involved with powering the ship. Fred's computer is not sophisticated enough to perform this function. Therefore, we will have to wait until someone can provide the additional technology required to accomplish this.

My second thought created an immediate response. Yes, this crop circle was introducing us to a new facet of the formations. Specific, physical structure was being communicated here. This crop circle was intended to be deciphered on a computer and transformed into a three-dimensional drawing.

These thoughts spilled over into my third and final brainstorm. What was this thing? My only answer was that it depicted a portion of the power plant. Exactly what function I do not know. I offer this astounding diagram to you and to our scientists to unravel the mystery within it.

Diagram No. 48: 3D Drawing of Model

Diagram No. 49: (E97+)

Now, let's move on to another puzzle within the crop circles. Is this the element used to power the ship? Take a look at Diagram 49. These figures were drawn in a Kansas field during the summer of 1991. They were immediately eradicated by the U. S. Government, attesting to their importance. If the number 97 is an atomic element, that element is berkelium (Bk), which has an atomic weight of 247 — pretty heavy. I believe the answer is Yes. It is the element used to power the ship. I will leave it up to our scientists to understand the meaning of the letter "E" and the "+" sign. It is possible that all of these figures have an entirely different meaning in higher mathematics, chemistry, or nuclear physics. At any rate, here is a gimme if there ever was one.

This completes my discussion of the ship's power plant. I am fully aware that I have created more questions than I answered, which is unavoidable at this time.

CHAPTER TWELVE

The Conclusion or the Beginning?

To me, what I have presented here is only the beginning. In closing this book, however, I offer a little assistance or guidelines for anyone wanting to pursue the crop circles further, particularly our scientists.

1) By the end of the 1995 summer season there will be at least a hundred virgin crop circles to decipher, including many that were undeciphered from 1992, 1993, and 1994. The majority of these formations address the power plant and the power source, or the particles involved. With the publication and distribution of this book, interest will increase. Access to diagrams of crop circles will, hopefully, be more easily attained. Accordingly, compiling all the diagrams of these formations should be a high priority. A few of these are presented for you to view in Diagrams 50-57 on the next two pages.

2) As you peruse these new formations, I suggest that you zero in on the simple ones and ignore the complex. This is what I did and it worked very well. Remember, the simple formations contain the information required to decipher the complex ones. In this instance there is an entire language pertaining to nuclear physics being conveyed. Once understood, the complex formations will be a snap to decipher.

3) If you reach an impasse while attempting to understand the information conveyed, just drop it for a while. I left the crop circles for a month once and returned to discover that my problem had disappeared. This is important advice, as you will come to understand.

4) Share your information with others. The crop circle creators drew their diagrams in fields to convey their intent that everyone should have access to them. If you seek the information within the crop circles for any reason other than for pure knowledge, I believe you will be thwarted.

5) Do not attempt to create rules with which to decipher the formations. They are teaching us a perfected method of investigation that

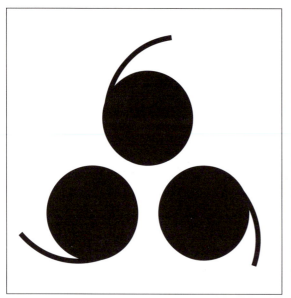

Diagram No. 50

Diagram No. 51

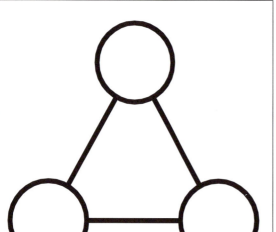

Diagram No. 52

Diagram No. 53

Diagram No. 54

Diagram No. 55

Diagram No. 56

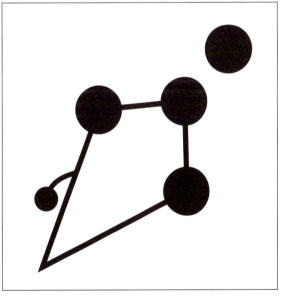

Diagram No. 57

can be applied to scientific research. I learned this lesson the hard way and amassed over two hundred rules, sub rules and sub-sub rules just within the first ten crop circles in this book. I ended up throwing the whole mess out. Address the formations by applying learned knowledge to them, and then let them lead you. I am telling you to incorporate intuition within your approach.

6) Use the crop circles to their utmost. They are the equivalent of a tool. Let them do the work for you. They will lead you to the correct conclusions so easily that you won't believe it. Conversely, do not wander off with your own theories. Stick to the formations. This is easier said than done.

7) At some point during your involvement with the crop circles you will discover what extraordinary teachers the creators of the crop circles are. You will also obtain an insight into how they think. If you ever harbored any fear about the whole thing, it will disappear. You will realize how caring these beings are. Share these thoughts with others. It is important.

8) Let's not repeat a previous mistake. No hoaxes, no disinformation, no deception! Openness, honesty, and the sharing of information are the order of the day.

9) Have fun doing this. Be happy! They did, and they expect you to. I am telling you that during my investigation of the crop circles I have detected a humorous personality.

SO. . . WHAT'S IT ALL ABOUT?

For as long as we have existed on our planet we have been unaware of the existence of extraterrestrial life forms. We have essentially been left alone to chart our own course without interference. Now, all of a sudden, we have visitors! To top it off, they are introducing themselves in a manner we never imagined. Our culture has nurtured the image of a space ship descending on the White House lawn with alien beings emerging. Instead, we get just the opposite — loving, compassionate, respectful folks who have taken extraordinary measures to ensure that they don't scare us! But why did they select such a phenomenal means of contact?

I believe it is because they perceive us as a fragmented society — which is a correct perception. We have many religions, many languages, many races and many cultures. They could not find a common denominator that applied to all of us. Therefore, they chose a hay field. That reminds me — Did you notice that by using a hay field, they included the planet itself within the communication loop? This is real class. This is respect that you and I have forgotten. We are going to learn a lot from these folks!

The bottom line is that as we continue to study and talk about the crop circles, we will actually be conversing about extraterrestrials who ARE HERE! We will, as a people, become more and more accustomed to the idea of their presence. When our mass consciousness fully accepts their existence, we will be ready to meet them. It will not happen one moment sooner.

The crop circle creators are full of feelings, emotions, love, compassion, and respect. They are extraterrestrials of the light — not aliens. I promise you this.

Relax. This is going to be an exciting and joyful journey for all of us. We, the living humans representing past generations of all humanity, are about to be inducted into the cosmic community some refer to as *The Light*. It is a wonderful time to be alive.

How The Photos Were Made

When Doug explained the type of photographs needed for *"The Gift"*, we both agreed that we should do a test to determine the proper lighting and film exposure. Doug had created a device constructed from an electric fan motor which we used to spin the models. The machine was set to work at low speed. Tungsten lights of 150 watts were set on each side of the model. We shielded the background from the influence of these lights.

The camera used was a Hasselblad CM with 80mm lens, set on a tripod. Polaroid film was used in a film holder attached to the Hasselblad to check the lighting and motion effect created by the spinning model.

I used a 400 ASA speed film with a shutter speed of 1/2 second and aperture set to F/11 and shutter speed of one second. After processing the test rolls, making contact sheets and some prints, we were ready to go ahead with completion of the photographs published in *"The Gift"*.

Rob Downey (left) and the author photographing a model.